Conrad's Endings
A Study of the Five Major Novels

Studies in Modern Literature, No. 39

A. Walton Litz, General Series Editor

Other Titles in This Series

No. 40	*Theories of Action in Conrad*	Francis A. Hubbard
No. 41	*The Ludic Imagination: A Study of the Play Element in Conrad's Literature*	Kenneth Simons
No. 42	*Conrad's Rebels: The Psychology of Revolution in the Novels from "Nostromo" to "Victory"*	Helen Funk Rieselbach
No. 43	*Conrad's Heroism*	Michael P. Jones
No. 46	*The Making of* Romance	Raymond Brebach
No. 47	*The* Nouvelle *of Henry James in Theory and Practice*	Lauren T. Cowdery
No. 48	*Women, Manners, and Morals: Henry James's Plays and the Comedy of Manners on the Turn-of-the-Century British Stage*	Susan Carlson
No. 49	*An International Act: Henry James and the Problem of Audience*	Anne Throne Margolis

Conrad's Endings
A Study of the Five Major Novels

by
Arnold E. Davidson
Professor of English
Michigan State University
East Lansing, Michigan

Produced and distributed by
UMI Research Press
an imprint of
University Microfilms International
A Xerox Information Resources Company
Ann Arbor, Michigan 48106

Library of Congress Cataloging in Publication Data

Davidson, Arnold E., 1936-
Conrad's endings.

(Studies in modern literature ; no. 39)
Revision of thesis (Ph.D.)–State University of New York at Binghamton, 1976.
Bibliography: p.
Includes index.
1. Conrad, Joseph, 1857-1924–Criticism and interpretation. 2. Closure (Rhetoric) 3. Fiction–Technique. I. Title. II. Series.
PR6005.O4Z657 1984 823'.912 84-8508
ISBN 0-8357-1587-6

For my Mother and Father

Contents

Acknowledgments *ix*

Introduction *1*

1 The Abdication of Lord Jim *7*

2 Patterns in *Nostromo* *31*

3 Levels of Plotting in *The Secret Agent* *55*

4 Deluded Vision in *Under Western Eyes* *71*

5 Limited Triumphs in *Victory* *87*

Notes *103*

Bibliography *119*

Index *123*

Acknowledgments

I am indebted to Professors Robert Kroetsch and John Hagan and the late William Bysshe Stein for their sustained encouragement and considerate counsel while I was writing the first version of this book. The State University of New York at Binghamton and the Canada Council provided me with much appreciated fellowships which partly funded that project and for which I again thank them. I would also like to thank the editors of *ARIEL: A Review of International English Literature, Conradiana, International Fiction Review,* and *Modern British Literature* for permitting me to revise and incorporate in the present book material previously published in those journals. I appreciate, too, the excellent work of my two typists, Randy McTeague (who prepared the original manuscript) and Mrs. Betty Uphaus (who did the revisions). Finally, my wife, Dr. Cathy N. Davidson, has shared in every phase of my work on Conrad, and it is to her that I am most indebted.

Introduction

A Beginning in Which Little is Concluded

To begin with endings is to entertain from the first some finally unanswerable questions. Not the least of these is a simple problem of definition and delineation: where does any beginning end and its complementary ending begin? Nor is the problem resolved by reintroducing the Aristotelian "middle" excluded from this bipolar posing of a dual question as to the structure and teleology, for the middle, mediating between the beginning and the end, only further blurs the confusion between them. Three terms are no less arbitrary and indistinct than two. In other words, the ending of the beginning and the beginning of the end as well as the verging into or out of the intervening middle are all conterminous throughout the text. Thus, as J. Hillis Miller has emphasized, "any point the spectator focuses on is a turning which both ties and unties," and this "is another way of saying that no narrative can show either its beginning or its ending" since "it always begins and ends still *in media res.*"[1]

Even if we could map out a certain textual space and clearly mark it — "Here there is ending" — another problem at once intrudes. Do we see within this boundary a living, breathing ending or only the appearance of one, a cunning simulacrum crafted by the author to imitate the real thing? Marianna Torgovnick, in her recent book *Closure in the Novel,* recognizes this problem but does not at all resolve it. "Closure," she writes, is "effective closure," and "the test [presumably for effectiveness] is the honesty and the appropriateness of the ending's relationship to beginning and middle, not the degree of finality or resolution achieved by the ending."[2] But what is honesty in a text other than a measure of how well the text lies? And appropriate to whom? In short, Torgovnick doubly begs the question instead of defining the term. All works terminate; some triumphantly, some dying in their tracks, but any distinction between those two ostensibly very different conclusions is itself a subjective value judgment and no doubt reflects more an estimation of the quality of the whole work than an evaluation of the ending itself. Indeed, the ending cannot be evaluated by itself, but must be weighed in relationship to the whole work, which necessarily means evaluating the whole work.

Assuming, now, that we have delineated an ending and determined that it is real, effective, honest, and appropriate, how then do we describe it? Is it, to use the current terminology, an open or a closed ending? Yet the conclusion of a novel is never self-evidently open or closed in the same sense that a door or a window is. Furthermore, the figurative analogy of ending as aperture, when applied to any narrative, necessarily works in two contradictory ways that equally undermine the question ostensibly addressed. Every ending is open, for the reader who has just concluded a work has necessarily emerged through that ending to a time and a space beyond the text. For that same reader, however, the same ending is now necessarily closed. Looking back, we see the whole text standing inviolate and not some special entrance into the heart of its matter. Furthermore, to review the whole text is usually to reread it, which entails entering again through the front door, not the back. But of course texts can be entered at any point. We can go through the ending again or we can mentally review and reweigh it to decide if it closes off or expands upon the material of the narration. And with the conclusion reread and reconsidered, we have still another question: is a revolving door open or closed?

The same inescapable indistinction that I have just posited has been differently argued by other critics. Torgovnick, for example, points out that, "from the beginning . . ., the term 'open' ending was an unfortunate one." As she rightly observes: "Every novel, including an 'open' one, establishes by its ending a 'closed' network of internal relationships." Furthermore, "even endings that produce a feeling of finality, as most endings involving a shift in time scale do, may be relatively 'open' or relatively 'closed' when compared to similar endings." Finally, as Torgovnick also argues, "the application of the terms 'open' and 'closed' can sometimes be very much a matter of interpretation."[3] One critic's closure is another's opening. And Miller even more emphatically denies the possibility of differentiating between an open ending and a closed one. As he maintains in "The Problematic of Ending in Narrative," every conclusion both knots up some narrative threads and unknots others. Interpretation, moreover, must perpetually untie what is tied and tie together what is untied. The model here is not the open or shut door but the resonance structure basic to particle physics. "Knotted, unknotted — there is no way to decide between these images. The novelist and the critic of novels needs them both and needs them both at once, in an indeterminable oscillation."[4] Consequently, for Miller, "no novel can be unequivocally finished or for that matter unequivocally unfinished. Attempts to characterize [any] fiction . . . by its commitment to closure or to open-endedness are blocked from the beginning by the impossibility of ever demonstrating whether a given narrative is closed or open. Analysis of endings leads always, if carried far enough, to the paralysis of this inability to decide."[5]

Matters are still more complicated in that the very consideration as to whether a particular ending is open or closed is often the code formulation of a rather different question. Almost half a century ago David Daiches argued that the modern novel (an ambiguous term then as now) was differentiated from earlier works in both content and form. Formally experimental fiction of the twentieth century, he suggested, "represents an attempted adjustment between literature and a certain state of transition in civilization and culture generally and . . . this adjustment explains most of the differentiating features of the twentieth-century novel."[6] More recently, Alan Friedman has developed Daiches's tentative proposition into a full-fledged theory of fictional modernity. In *The Turn of the Novel,* Friedman maintains that "the 'open' pattern of the novel came into being because it reflected and conveyed a new attitude toward the process and goals of experience in life."[7] Friedman explicitly insists that "the expanding and then narrowing flux of conscience as the pattern of the novel is a powerful assumption that underlies virtually the entire canon of English fiction from Defoe and Richardson to . . . the early novels of the twentieth century."[8] But with the disintegration and disorder that characterize much of the facts of the twentieth century, certain changes took place in the fiction too. "The process of experience which underlay the novel was itself disrupted and reorganized. The new flux of experience insisted on a new vision of existence: it stressed an ethical vision of continual expansion and virtually unrelieved openness in the experience of life."[9] Narratively indeterminant endings, "open endings," came into fashion, whereas the eighteenth and nineteenth centuries, with their more stable systems of belief, produced fictions that were fixed, controlled, "closed." An open ending is thus a modern ending, so much so that to ask if the ending is open is to ask if the novel is modern.[10] In effect, however, what Friedman actually posits is a tight little circle of definition, periodization, and evaluation: open endings are modern endings; modern endings are better endings; better endings are open endings.

Yet the same open ending that demonstrates, to some critics, a text's modern provenance demonstrates to others its author's deficient art. Members of the Chicago school have especially argued, to borrow two relevant titles, that if the novel enfolds both fiction and the shape of belief, then the rhetoric of fiction must speak to that informing belief. Such teleology demands its end. This whole view of endings is most fully expressed by David H. Richter, who, in *Fable's End: Completeness and Closure in Rhetorical Fiction,* simply refuses to accept literary openness as a special feature of modern fiction. "Within any system of public beliefs," Richter argues, "many aesthetic forms are possible, and acceptable conclusions to novels — ones which leave us with a sense of completeness — depend less upon the particular conventions of society than upon the kinds of instabilities which, once represented in a fiction, must be resolved."[11] For Richter, the "operative" term in "open form" is "form." So "however 'unlimited' the flux of experience portrayed, however expansive the ethical framework," the most wily novelists "have never quite managed to get around Aristotle's dictum that a work of art must be 'whole, complete, and of sufficient magnitude.' "[12] The novelists' failure attests, however, not to the dictates of form but to the nebulosity of the dictum. If it looks like art and is "whole, complete and of sufficient magnitude," it is a work of art. It is a work of art, and — look! — it is "whole, complete, and of sufficient magnitude." This is an older circle than Friedman's but as empty quite. The open ending as debit is no less indefinite and problematic than is the open ending as credit.

There is duplicity even in the description of the undelineateable ending. But the conclusion as a critical crux perhaps reflects a still deeper problem, the conclusion as a teleological crux. Essentially, any narrative ending necessarily throws into focus the contradictory nature of the two main ends served by narrative. The novel is mimetic; we expect to encounter in fiction versions of the world in which we live. The novel is also a literary form; we expect the vision of life reflected in the text to be mediated into a work of art. These two impulses or ends — to portray and to pattern — are most in conflict at the work's conclusion. Consider, for example (since this paragraph is already heavy with mirror metaphors), Stendahl's famous image of the novel as "a mirror carried along a high road."[13] No mirror, however reflective, can conceivably go on forever. And whatever the conclusion, some obvious gesture of closure (a bow or a pirouette — a horizontal or vertical scanning of the landscape) or simply an inobtrusive end to progress, the mirror at rest is qualitatively different from the mirror in motion. In short, the termination always announces itself as something other than the continuation. As Frank Kermode cogently observes, despite whatever freedoms are granted in and to the narrative, "the novel has its end."[14] A finality not found in real life is authorially imposed, and consequently the novel "has to lie."

The novelist's problem is summed up by Henry James in his preface to *Roderick Hudson:* "Really, universally, relations stop nowhere, and the exquisite problem of the artist is eternally but to draw, by a geometry of his own, the circle within which they shall happily *appear* to do so."[16] This problem can be resolved in different ways. "If it was not for death and marriage," E.M. Forster observes, "I do not know how the average novelist would conclude."[17] More elegant solutions can entail a direct confrontation with the difficulty of ending, as in the last chapter of Samuel Johnson's *Rasselas* "in which nothing is concluded" or the deliberately oblique conclusions of Laurence Sterne's *Tristram Shandy* (we are told at the end that it has all been a story about "a COCK and a BULL") and Herman Melville's *The Confidence Man* (we are told at the end that "something further may follow of this masquerade"). Or the problem can be avoided entirely, which is exactly what James Joyce achieves by working *Finnegans Wake* into a narrative circle, one with no beginning or end at all. Still other writers focus on the duplicity of James's *"appear"* by providing alternate conclusions, as does Charles Dickens in *Great Expectations* with its two different endings or John Fowles in *The French Lieutenant's Woman* with three. The record here is no doubt held by Richard Brautigan, whose *A Confederate General from Big Sur* spins to a close with "more and more endings: the sixth, the 53rd, the 131st, the 9,435th ending, endings going faster and faster, more and more endings, faster and faster until this book is having 186,000 endings per second."[18] There are limits even in this relativistic universe.

Conrad's solution is no less elegant than any of these.[19] As I will argue in the subsequent chapters, each of his five major novels achieves a characteristically Conradian sense of ending by incorporating into its conclusion the very impossibility of conclusion that necessarily compromises the task of writing an ending or of writing definitively about one.[20]

1

The Abdication of Lord Jim

A study of Conrad's endings can appropriately begin with an examination of the conclusion to *Lord Jim* and not just because this particular novel is one of its author's first major works. It is also a text that terminates in a particularly problematic fashion. Suresh Raval, for example, in a recent essay, first quotes most of the last three paragraphs of the novel and then assesses their narrative function: "These are Marlow's concluding words of the story of Jim's life, of his own response to Jim; they also end *Lord Jim.* But they do not signal for Marlow a conclusive response to Jim, nor do they signal for the reader the possibility of a reading that would decipher both the meaning of Jim's life and the meaning of *Lord Jim* in an unambiguous mode. The ending," Raval continues, "is a compound of poignancy, confidence, and uncertainty perhaps best characterized as profoundly disturbed and disturbing ambivalence."[1] That ambivalence cannot be dispelled, but the grounds of its origin can be mapped in the novel. Another recent critic notes that "Conrad's novels . . . are subjected to a process of unobtrusive but systematic patterning."[2] As I will subsequently argue, it is this very patterning in the novel that throws the unclear issues of the conclusion into sharper focus.[3]

There is still another reason for carefully weighing both the text's and its eponymous protagonist's conclusion. A conventional reading of the latter has established a conventional reading of the former. More simply put, Lord Jim's death in Patusan has frequently been regarded as final proof that this character at last achieves heroic status and thereby vindicates his earlier failures to conform to his own high ideals. Robert Haugh, for example, maintains that when Jim chooses "honor and death" he "redeems himself magnificently."[4] Jocelyn Baines similarly claims that even though "some critics have asserted that Jim's life ended in defeat . . . there can be little doubt that Conrad approved of Jim's [final] action."[5] Others have even fewer misgivings about this "lord's" last deeds. His passive death at the hand of Doramin, Elliott Gose argues, in appropriately soaring terms, is more an apotheosis than a suicide: "By sacrificing his physical body to his concept of himself, Jim has finally freed himself for good from the mud and filth of the temporal world." He has "flown to the height of the stars, become the high light he longed to be."[6] In much that same vein, Ted Boyle also suggests that Jim "gains immortality by his last unselfish act."[7] Or Ian Watt concludes his recent extended analysis of the novel's conclusion by positing a more modest elevation. This critic sees Jim as the only "hero of a great twentieth-century novel" who achieves "nobility" by dying, in best aristocratic fashion, "for his honor."[8] As Paul Bruss observes, "it is clear that a majority of Conrad scholars have enthusiastically subscribed to the view that Jim in Patusan does enjoy a triumph."[9]

Thus interpreted, *Lord Jim* is an account of how a hero's preliminary falterings end in final victory. But must we then agree with Commodore Sir Ivan Thompson who finds in Jim's story "a rousing and edifying tale of adventure" that tells how "a decent boy makes one slip, but makes good, and in the end makes the supreme sacrifice"?[10] "Making" one slip to then "make good" — particularly through some "supreme sacrifice" — makes for rather old-fashioned fiction. Furthermore, it would be most ironic, ironic at the expense of the author, if *Lord Jim* itself was ultimately the same kind of "light holiday literature" that led its protagonist to discover "his vocation for the sea" and thus launched him upon his confused career.[11] Surely Conrad's novel is not the "edifying tale" that the Commodore describes, and a careful assessment of its conclusion does not show Jim at last fulfilling the visions first fostered by "the sea-life of light literature" (p. 6). Jim finds his end in his beginning in quite a different fashion. Indeed, by examining the manner in which his visions of himself are finally extinguished, we should see that Jim, even in dying, fails one more time to be the man whom he would die to be.

The conclusion of the novel also demonstrates that Jim, in Patusan, was not the reestablished hero Marlow occasionally posits during his long narration assessing the cause and consequences of Jim's jump from the *Patna*. The middle section of the book, chapters five through thirty-five, contain a number of such statements as, "My last words about Jim shall be few. I affirm he had achieved greatness" (p. 225). But these seemingly definitive affirmations of another's "greatness" are compromised in both their immediate and their general context. The assertion just quoted, for example, comes directly after Marlow admits "the last word is not said — probably never shall be said" (p. 225). Any attempt then to provide some last word must be unconvincing, particularly when it is followed by thousands of additional words. In other ways too Conrad indicates that Marlow does not unreservedly accept his own explicit pronouncements about Jim's postulated Patusan success. The narrator, as apologist, may describe his protégé journeying upriver towards "greatness as genuine as any man ever achieved" (p. 244). He can promise Jewel that she will never, as she fears, be abandoned, because Jim, he claims, is "better" and "more true" than other men (p. 314). But pressed on that point, Marlow soon sounds a different note and "brutally" informs the girl that Jim will never be called away from her "because he is not good enough" (p. 318). The visiting captain cannot exorcise (his term) Jewel's doubts about Jim because he cannot exorcise his own. As he at that point in his story confesses: "For my part, I cannot say what I believed — indeed I don't know to this day, and never shall probably" (p. 320). Nevertheless, only a few pages later, he is again assuring his anonymous auditors that he has again "made up [his] mind that Jim . . . had at last mastered his fate" (p. 324). No wonder they are not convinced at the end of the narration and silently depart, "as if the last image of that incomplete story, its incompleteness itself, and the very tone of the speaker, had made discussion vain and comment impossible" (p. 337).

The silence of these unnamed auditors speaks of — to quote one of Conrad's most perceptive contemporary critics — "something suspect in Marlow's enterprise of interpretation."[12] As Edward Said has recently observed, the novel is "essentially [a] retrospective and investigative inquiry."[13] That investigation is conducted, of course, by Marlow, who early recognizes that "you can't expect the constituted authorities to inquire into the state of a man's soul" (pp. 56-57) and neither can you expect the culprit in question to carry out that same task — "for it is my belief no man even understands quite his own artful dodges to escape from the grim shadow of self-knowledge" (p. 80). But Marlow himself is not above suspicion either, especially as it becomes clear that in his inquiry into Jim's case he functions as an odd combination of judge and jury, advocate and prosecuting attorney, expert witness and court reporter. Moreover, as the novel progresses, the role of advocate increasingly predominates, and Jim becomes more Marlow's protégé than the object of his dispassionate investigation. Thus the older captain is often indulgent in his evaluations of the younger man, occasionally overlooks the implications of specific details when recounting what Jim did or did not do, and even engages in some special pleading. This blurring of roles puts Marlow's trial on trial. In other words, Conrad, with consummate skill, controls the manner in which his narrator renders his account and thereby provides numerous clues that allow the reader to judge Jim rather differently than Marlow does. The resultant double focus especially pervades the concluding chapters of the book, for here Marlow's claims for Jim are most at odds with the account of his actions. An examination of the ending of *Lord Jim* can therefore serve as a good introduction to the novel as a whole. Certainly such a study should dispel the claim (which not even Marlow will finally unequivocally assert) that Jim comes to "achieve the final success of heroic death."[14]

Marlow, even as he concludes his long spoken narration, suggests that he is not so certain of the former mate's present success as he had previously claimed to be. He describes how, after visiting Patusan, he last saw Jim, a "white figure" that "seemed to stand at the heart of a vast enigma"; that dwindled, in the darkening twilight, into "a tiny white speck" which was "suddenly . . . lost" (p. 336). That disappearing speck is not fully commensurate with previous claims of "greatness as genuine as any man ever achieved" (p. 244). Looking back in the ominously suggestive gathering dusk on a dark coast that then "seemed the very stronghold of the night" (p. 335), Marlow wondered if that young romantic's "opportunity" might not yet be "by his side — still veiled." "Was it still veiled?" he then asks, to answer simply, "I don't know" (p. 336). That response evokes Marlow's earlier description of how Jim first entered Patusan. Marlow then pictured him, in a native canoe, sitting on "his tin box, nursing the unloaded revolver on his lap," while his "opportunity sat veiled by his side like an Eastern bride waiting to be uncovered by the hand of the master" (p. 243-44). Obviously, as Marlow unwittingly admits during the course of his spoken narration, so far as he knows, the bride is still veiled. Therefore any claims set forth in that narration about Jim's final condition, including those of Jim himself — "I believe I am equal to all my luck!" (p. 304) or, "I shall hold what I've got. Can't expect anything more" (p. 333) — are necessarily premature.

The third and last section of the book attests to the validity of Jewel's prophetic doubts, of Marlow's half-repressed misgivings, of the unnamed auditors' more obvious skepticism. As J.E. Tanner argues, the claims advanced in the middle section of the novel about its protagonist's final success must be seen as "the hopeful conclusions of a Marlow immensely pleased with the achievements of Jim whom he has recently visited for a month in Patusan."[15] Marlow, Tanner also notes, has been similarly satisfied before. When he received his friend, Mr. Denver's, first letter, he "was trebly pleased — at Jim's shaping so well, at the tone of the letter, at [his] own cleverness" and congratulated himself that he "had known what [he] was doing" and "had read characters aright" (p. 188). He even starts to construct for Jim "a castle in Spain," a dream of the young man becoming the older man's heir. That dream, however, is soon dispelled by the same friend's second letter and the news of Jim's decamping. Obviously Marlow can be wrong in his estimations of Jim's success. Indeed, on the basis of a carefully constructed chronology, Tanner points out that, "ironically," Marlow is probably presenting his account of Jim's victory — "a victory in which [he] had taken [his] part" (p. 244) — "only shortly before Jim's death."[16] In other words, as an earlier critic succinctly observed, "most of the narrative of Jim's history [and redemption] is told before all the facts are in."[17]

The narrator soon finds out that his first assessment of the subject of his story is no longer tenable. Most of the final section of the novel is his written account of how "accident, hazard, Fortune," (p. 320), and, more specifically, Gentleman Brown helped to uncover the true visage of Jim's destiny. There is, Marlow claims in his letter accompanying that narration, "a sort of profound and terrifying logic" (p. 342) to the process whereby the metaphoric veil previously present was finally stripped away. Jim, with "his last proud and unflinching glance" (p. 416), perhaps had a momentary view of what his fate must be. As Marlow at the end of his penned narration (and at the conclusion of the novel) writes, "it well may be that . . . he had beheld the face of that opportunity which, like an Eastern bride, had come veiled to his side" (p. 416). If so, what was the nature of the bride and how was the veil removed?

"It all begins, as I've told you, with the man called Brown" (p. 352). Thus Marlow begins his second narration, the written account of Jim's end that he pens for "the privileged man" (p. 337) and with which he tries to penetrate "the profound and terrifying logic" (p. 342) that still underlies, for him, Jim's death. But even in this beginning there is an implicit suggestion that Marlow does not intend. At this point in the novel, the reader — any reader of the novel and the privileged man — has seen enough of Jim's past career to suspect that some coming disaster cannot possibly all begin with Brown. That suspicion is soon verified. As Marlow goes on to describe in some detail Brown's role in Jim's tragedy, he does so in terms that regularly suggest Jim's larger role in that same disaster. With unconscious echoes from his earlier narration, with parallels the point of which he overlooks, with phrasings that imply meanings other than those he wishes to advance, Marlow, in his second narration, as in his first one, does not paint quite the picture he would prefer to present.

Brown, for example, in a disastrous situation, "stole with complete success a Spanish schooner out of a small bay near Zamboanga" (p. 344). Then, after the raiding expedition to Patusan had been foiled and he and his men again face death, Brown condemns Jim for being "so damnedly hard upon a man trying to get out of a deadly hole by the first means that came to hand" (p. 387) and thereby effectively pursues the one course of action that promises any chance of escape. He proclaims (and he demonstrates, too, the truth of that proclamation) that he would not "leave" his men "in a d--d lurch" (p. 383). Marlow, writing a retrospective narration, will eventually describe how Jim did jump and with that final leap left all those he proclaimed himself to be responsible for in precisely that "d--d lurch." In brief, from the very beginning of Marlow's final narration, Conrad contrasts Brown's shrewd attempts to save both himself and his men with Jim's imperceptive miscalculations and immobilizing torpidity in roughly similar situations.[18]

A second implicit contrast also occurs early in Marlow's written narrative. Brown, at one point in his career, "ran off — it was reported — with the wife of a missionary, a very young girl from Clapham way, who had married the mild, flat-footed fellow in a moment of enthusiasm, and suddenly transported to Melanesia, lost her bearings somehow" (p. 353). With this at first apparently irrelevant bit of biographical gossip, Conrad contrives to have two young ladies "lost" in Melanesia. Marlow does not compare the English girl's situation to Jewel's. He merely summarizes the way in which the former's "dark story" ended, but he does so almost immediately after he has just described, in the last part of his letter to the privileged man, the final result of another dark story, Jewel's inconsolable grief at being abandoned by a Jim who had become to her and her pleas, "blind and deaf and without pity" (p. 349). That placing allows the reader to equate the two cases. Brown tried to save the women he loved. After she had contracted a serious illness, he was attempting to carry her away when she "died on board his ship," whereupon he uncharacteristically "gave way to an outburst of sombre and violent grief" (p. 353). Jim, however, leaves Jewel to lament an injury she can neither comprehend nor forgive while she sinks into a frozen death-in-life existence.[19]

It might also be noted that Jim's ties to Jewel are rather more substantial than were Brown's to the English girl. The outlaw, after all, merely ran off with another man's wife who soon died afterwards. The most we might say is that he at least had the courage of his immoral romantic inclinations. Jim, however, literally owed his life to Jewel and had totally committed himself to her. Marlow earlier described how, soon after Jim arrived in Patusan, the young woman began to spend her nights watching over the newcomer too naive to appreciate the danger he confronted and thereby saved him from an attempted assassination. He also told how Jim described his devotion to Jewel: "You take a different view of your actions when you come to understand, when you are *made* to understand every day that your existence is necessary — you see, absolutely necessary — to another person" (p. 304). For Jim, Jewel, like Patusan, "was a trust," and he claimed to Marlow, "I believe I am equal to it . . . I believe I am equal to all my luck!" (p. 304). Jewel herself also informs Marlow that Jim "swore he would never leave me, when we stood there alone! He swore to me!" (p. 313). But she knows that "other men," both her father and her mother's father, for example, "had sworn the same thing" (p. 314) and then proved false. The basis of her fear is the tragic fate of her mother, deserted by her father (who may have been Stein).[20] She does not want to die like her mother, weeping. But she will be deserted too to be consigned, at the end of the novel, to a kind of life in death. In at least one respect, his dealings with the women he supposedly loved, the outlaw was consideraby truer than the lord.

A more obvious illustration of Conrad compromising what his narrator reports is seen when Brown charges Jim with being "so damnedly hard upon a man trying to get out of a deadly hole by the first means that came to hand" (p. 387). The outlaw, as earlier noted, insists that, with his "men in the same boat," he was "not the sort to jump out of trouble and leave them in a d--d lurch" (pp. 382-83). Such phrasing must recall Jim's failure on the *Patna*, a failure which, as critics of the novel have long observed, prompts in Jim a "crippling identification with Gentleman Brown" that soon leads to tragedy.[21] For Marlow, however, the disaster does not derive from Jim's past still manifesting itself in a mental and spiritual collapse effected by a challenge to his probity: "No, he [Brown] didn't turn Jim's soul inside out" (p. 385). Instead, Marlow blames the whole matter on Brown's dark powers — on his "satanic gift of finding out the best and the weakest spot [it is curious that they should be the same] in his victim" (p. 385) — and on his perceptiveness, "as if a demon had been whispering advice in his ear" (pp. 386-87). Brown's perspicacity clearly contributes to his success, but that does not explain the effect of his words on Jim.

Even though Brown effects the collapse of Jim's venture in Patusan, Marlow, describing the crucial meeting between these two Europeans and the consequences of that encounter, often either overlooks the implications of specific details in his story or sees them darkly, through the glass of his own attempts to idealize his image of Jim. For example, Cornelius twice figures prominently in situations in which Jim could well have been killed. He "played a very dubious part" (p. 285) in the assassination attempt that occurred soon after Jim reached Patusan and that was forestalled mostly through Jewel's watchful dedication. He advises Brown, while that outlaw awaits Jim's return to the armed town, to conquer Patusan by simply shooting Jim, who will come, Cornelius rightly predicts, to parley with the bandits. In both cases Cornelius exhibits "unsuspected [by Marlow as well as Jim] depths of cunning" (p. 344). But only in the first episode does Marlow also see some of the evidence that "demonstrated Jim's absurd carelessness" (p. 285).

The evidence, in the first case, is obvious. Marlow describes how Jim, who "had got the Bugis irretrievably committed to action and had made himself responsible for success on his own head" (p. 296), also insisted on risking his life by not remaining with the Bugis. "With an utter disregard of his personal safety" (p. 285), he had recrossed the river over which he had recently escaped to reside on the side controlled by the Rajah. He remained there, Marlow also notes, despite rumors that he was going to be killed and when much more was at issue than his own safety. The same point, incidentally, is demonstrated on a more mundane level by Jim's monthly partaking of the Rajah's coffee. The former mate viewed this regularly repeated ritual as an act supposedly proving that "personally he thought nothing of poison" (p. 250). Marlow, participating in one of these visits, more reasonably sees the whole venture as "a stupid risk" (p. 250).

The evidence of Jim's carelessness should be just as obvious in the second case, which is substantially a reenactment of the first one. Thus the abject Cornelius, not really particularly shrewd, can foresee that Jim, who has previously shown a certain cavalier disregard for his own welfare and for what might happen to Patusan if he were killed, will do so again: "He shall come to talk to you . . . . Yes. He will come straight here and talk to you" (p. 377). Cornelius obviously knows Jim better than Jim or Marlow knows Cornelius. This abject man was earlier described by Marlow as "too insignificant to be dangerous" (p. 326). That assessment is at odds with the dangerously astute counsel Cornelius twice tries to persuade Brown to accept. "All you have to do is kill him and then you are king here," he first advises (p. 368), and later, even more explicitly, "Just you kill him, and you shall frighten everybody so much that you can do anything you like with them afterwards — get what you like — go away when you like" (p. 378).

Perhaps because he once joined his protégé in a cup of coffee that well might have been poisoned, Marlow, in his first narration, can condemn Jim's monthly calls on the Rajah as a foolish flirting with death. But he does not criticize Jim, in his second narration, for paying an even more dangerous visit on Brown. Furthermore, the Rajah really is too comic a villain to be taken completely seriously, whereas Brown, as a villain, is a deadly serious threat from the moment of his first arrival. Indeed, both Marlow and Jim should have seen something of the nature of Brown and should have recognized the danger to Jim and his people if Jim, in any way, put himself in Brown's power. And claims such as "no direct incriminating evidence against Brown is available" are clearly mistaken.[22] Brown had his Yankee "dead shot" gratuitously bring down a distant Bugis man simply because "that showed them what we could do" (p. 371). Jim, however, remains oblivious to the implications of this demonstration when he arrives in person to confer with Brown. Although he had once attempted to imagine what Patusan would be without him and seen it simply as "hell loose" (p. 333), he now pointlessly risks his life instead of sending some emissary or simply proceeding to dispose of the outlaws.

It is clear that Jim, in coming to confer with Brown, has put his life at risk. Marlow describes how the outlaw leader at once informed his antagonist that they were both equally "dead" because one of Brown's men "had a bead drawn on him all the time, and only waited for a sign" that he should shoot (p. 381). But the author's irony is implicit in what his narrator merely reports. Marlow goes on to tell of Jim's answer to Brown's observation that the trapped rat can bite. "Not if you don't near the trap till the rat is dead," the younger man, with almost comic obtuseness, retorts, quite unaware that he had just, "of his own free will," walked into the trap and joined the rat (p. 381).

"They met," Marlow wrote, "where Jim took the second desperate leap of his life — the leap that landed him into the life of Patusan, into the trust, the love, the confidence of the people" (pp. 379-80). The place is appropriate. When Brown and his raiding party arrived in Patusan to meet their first setback at the hands of the forewarned natives, Dain Waris, who had directed that initial repulse, "wished to settle the business off-hand, but his people were too much for him" (p. 361). Because he lacked "Jim's racial prestige and the reputation of invincible, supernatural power" (p. 361), the other Bugis, armed and numerous enough to dispatch "the fourteen desperate invaders" (p. 360), insisted on awaiting Jim's return. Therefore, precisely because he had earlier led his native followers to their great victory over Sherif Ali, Jim is required to meet another demanding test. The leap in anticipates and even precipitates the leap out.

The direction of that second leap is also early indicated. When the two white men first "faced each other across the creek," they "with steady eyes tried to understand each other before they opened their lips" (p. 380). In this reciprocal endeavor, Brown is by far the more successful. With much evidence immediately at hand, Jim is still incapable of gaging his antagonist's character, while Brown, so he later told Marlow, "could see directly I set my eyes on him what sort of a fool he was" (p. 344). Marlow himself partly validates the other's judgment of Jim when he writes that "Brown, as though he had been really great, had a satanic gift of finding out the best and the weakest spot in his victims" (p. 385). Consequently, even though Jim seemed to have "all the advantages on his side — possession, security, power" (p. 380), the confrontation that Marlow describes as "the deadliest kind of duel on which Fate looked on with her cold-eyed knowledge of the end" (p. 385) must end with Jim's defeat.

The meeting between the two, "the cynical Brown's unerring discovery of his antagonist's weakness," constitutes, Albert Guerard argues, "one of the great dramatic scenes in Conrad."[23] As such, it has been often assessed. But with this episode particularly, we see how ready various commentators are to follow Marlow's lead; to judge the book's protagonist rather leniently; and, in some cases, to put forward suggested explanations of Jim's motives that largely justify the tragedy that derives from his disastrous misestimation of Brown. Consider, for example, Walter Wright who, some thirty-five years ago, claimed that Jim "stakes his own life on the belief that his kindness to Brown has renewed his [Brown's] faith in humanity and will make him leave in peace." Wright thus concludes that Jim is guided by a "noble motive," his "belief in the human decency of even the most degraded."[24] This "belief" could be better described as blind supposition. Brown never evinces the slightest vestige of some "faith in humanity" that might be resurrected by Jim's kindness.

What Wright's apology really requires is that we respect Jim because he is, this critic suggests, ready to hazard his own life, the happiness of a loved one, and the welfare of many others whom he has promised to protect on the totally untested hypothesis that a hitherto vicious man has just undergone a moral reformation. Jim himself could hardly put forward a more flattering explanation of his failure. Yet such theories continue to be propounded. Jocelyn Baines later maintained that Jim "was by European standards right to let Brown and his men go; the offer of 'a clear road or else a clear fight' expressed the conviction of an honorable, civilized man."[25] Still more recently, Harry Epstein similarly lauded Jim for being "humane enough not to kill a man who is at his mercy."[26] Epstein, moreover, does not even require, as Wright did, that the supposed morality which prompts Jim to permit Brown to leave Patusan be premised on some hope that the latter has given up his evil ways: "For even had Jim recognized Brown's radically evil nature, it still would have been presumptuous to kill him once Jim has him at his mercy; without knowledge of the secret channel, Jim cannot know of any way for Brown to do harm."[27] Is it not, however, more presumptuous for Jim to assume he can safely release the "radically evil" with no guarantee — requiring them to surrender their guns, for example — that they will not at once proceed to act in accordance with their basic nature? And is he not inexcusably stupid to assume that a boatload of armed bandits set loose on a fogbound tidal river could not come up with some possible way to work willful mischief, if such is their intent? Surely the fog itself, one in which "nothing could be seen" (p. 399), provides "secret channel" enough.

"Yes, presently we shall see clear" (p. 398). These are almost the last words Jim hears Brown speak as the latter leaves Patusan in the symbolically suggestive fog that then "muffled" even his voice. As he predicted, Jim soon sees, if not clear, at least more clearly. He finally perceives that he has been wrong about Brown and has grossly miscalculated in providing the "clear road." But he should have seen sooner. There were ample clues all along, as is clearly indicated in Marlow's narrative. Marlow, however, seems to be most bemused by the problem of how Brown so readily apprehended the essential nature of his opponent — "it was as if a demon had been whispering advice in his ear" (pp. 386-87) — and never questions how Jim could remain so totally in the dark about Brown, despite the fact that the leader of the outlaws took no particular pains to conceal his essential nature and his savage animosity to all that in any way thwarted his desires: "I am not a coward. Don't you be one. Bring them along [the 'unoffending people' whom Brown admits he 'set upon' because he was starving, and whom he claims he now wants to engage in a clear fight] or, by all of the fiends, we shall yet manage to send half your unoffending town to heaven with us in smoke!" (p. 382).

Brown here directly expresses what the Bugis under Dain Waris and in the absence of their supposedly more capable white lord had no problem immediately discerning, that he and his men represented a definite danger to the town of Patusan. As he later acknowledged to Marlow, who sought him out to hear his dying confession (Marlow had industriously gathered much evidence but is not so industrious in his interpretation of it), "perceiving the size of the place, he [Brown] had resolved instantly in his mind that as soon as he had gained a footing he would set fire right and left." Then, as the conflagration raged, he would, "by shooting down everything living in sight," further "cow and terrify the population" (p. 386). Marlow thus knows that, "in truth, Dain Waris's energetic action had prevented the greatest calamities" (p. 386). But he never draws the comparison between Dain Waris's effective "energetic action" and Jim's fumbling and ineffectual attempts to cope with these same invaders.

Dain Waris averted one calamity. Jim's death would have caused another. Fortunately for both Jim and Patusan, Brown does not know just how well he has been advised by Cornelius. He apparently cannot believe that an "immense" town seemingly filled "with thousands of angry men" (p. 360) could be overcome by merely killing one man. What if the death of their leader only made those thousands more angry, more determined to avenge the injury they had suffered? An earlier act designed to show the natives what the white men could do hardly accomplished the end intended. When the Yankee "long shot" killed the distant townsmen, that act did not prompt a panic but led, instead, to a partial retaliation and an official declaration of war. A volunteer herald, creeping close to the outlaw camp, was able to wound mortally one of Brown's men before he delivered his message and "proclaimed that between the men of the Bugis nation living in Patusan and the white men on the hill..., there would be no faith, no compassion, no speech, no peace" (p. 375). And only the natives, we might notice, honestly declare their hostile intentions, as civilized peoples are supposed to do.

Jim obviously refused to be bound by the Bugis' proclamation of war. He comes in peace to speak to Brown, thereby endangering himself and the people he is pledged to protect. But Brown disregards Cornelius's counsel to pursue another policy which he hopes might save him and his men. And paradoxically, Brown's success in effecting his escape depends on Jim's evincing another of the qualities the Bugis had earlier proscribed. Those who have shown that they were without mercy now claim that they should be treated with some compassion. Then, when they are allowed to leave, they demonstrate how little they merited Jim's faith that they could be trusted to keep an implied agreement and depart in peace.[28] Brown, deprived "of a common robber's success," takes revenge with "an act of cold-blooded ferocity" (p. 403).

Brown's basic ploy is to propose that Jim choose between only two courses of action. "Give us a fight or a clear road to go back whence we came," he demands (p. 382). For himself, he similarly, and somewhat self-contradictorily, claims "the privilege to beg for the favour of being shot quickly, or else kicked out to go free and starve in my own way" (p. 383). Consequently, what Baines sees as the "conviction of an honorable, civilized man," Jim's promise that "you shall have a clear road or else a clear fight" (p. 388), is not a dichotomy enunciating Jim's principles at all. Neither critic nor character considers possibilities other than those suggested by Brown, who is distinguished for neither honor nor civility. Furthermore, they both overlook the fact that Brown himself is not at all interested in the first of his requested alternatives. He could, of course, obtain the favor of an open fight to the finish whenever he so desired. All he has to do is lead one last charge. But he earlier gave only "a passing thought" to the plan "of trying to rush the town." It would have served no purpose, for he and his men, "in the lighted street, . . . would be shot down like dogs" (p. 374).

There is still more to Brown's duplicity. Jim never notices how the outlaw regularly implies that if he shall not be allowed to go free, if they are to have a "clear fight" — his opponent is supposedly "to white" to let the "rat" simply die in the trap (p. 381) — then it will be fought on Brown's terms. He is to be assailed on his now fortified hill as opposed to his attacking the also barricaded town. In short, even while ostensibly putting the decision as to the outlaws' survival entirely in Jim's hands, Brown is staking out for himself the most advantageous field of battle should that decision go against him. Jim, naturally, fails to notice this conniving. Even more dubiously, he never asks why he should sacrifice the lives of any of his own people so that a band of outlaws might perish in the manner to which their leader claims they are entitled.

Jim also might have considered the moral implications of allowing Brown to leave Patusan. The outlaw's second alternative, "a clear road to go back whence we came" (p. 382), does suggest a pertinent consideration: To go back to do what? But Jim does not put that question to himself or to Brown and neither does he note that this same question is, in effect, unintentionally answered even though it was never asked. When Brown rephrases his two-term proposal, he insists that he would either be killed honorably (according to his own standards of honor, of course) or "kicked out to go free and *starve in my own fashion*" (p. 383, emphasis added). His presence in Patusan attests to the manner in which he and his men might be expected to starve. They will not be passive victims of misfortune when others can be victimized. As Brown himself admitted, attacking an "unoffending people" is nothing to him when he is starving "for next to no offence" (p. 382). Nevertheless, Brown, Jim, and various Conrad critics would all agree that even though he obviously came to Patusan to seize supplies (he never seriously attempts to beg, barter, or buy), this outlaw, with his armed men, is still entitled to depart unhindered so that he can try his luck at some similar venture elsewhere. The basis for Brown's belief that he should be allowed such a second chance is obvious, but it is difficult to comprehend why anyone else should agree with him.

Although he had clearly planned to plunder, Brown soon pretended that his intentions were more honorable. "As to coming to Patusan, who had the right to say he hadn't come to beg?" Marlow goes on to observe that Brown "made the point brazenly" (p. 386), as indeed he must. Witness again the shooting of the distant man. Brown necessarily glosses over this killing, and Jim allows him to do so. The Bugis, however, had no problem finding in that same act "an atrocity" and a cause for "bitter rage" (pp. 375-76). And the Bugis are right, for men honestly seeking assistance do not generally do so by going armed to isolated, out-of-the-way places where they then proceed to shoot their intended benefactors. Yet Jim only once seemingly senses that there is something dubious about Brown and his story. Having already half-decided that the outlaws shall be allowed a safe passage back down the river, Jim first inquires if they will "promise to leave the coast." When Brown assents, Jim then poses a second, more problematic stipulation: "And surrender your arms?" (p. 387). But any misgivings prompting that tentative second condition for Brown's release are immediately suppressed, and Jim allows Brown to settle the matter by categorically refusing: "Surrender our arms! Not till you come to take them out of our stiff hands. You think I am gone crazy with funk? Oh, no!" (p. 388).

Paul Kirschner argues that Brown's refusal to give up his weapons constitutes a "profession of courage" which Jim "must respect" as such "because he himself never admitted his cowardice on the *Patna*"[29] But Brown's professed determination to remain armed constitutes not a proof of his bravery but a refutation of his recent portrait of himself as a mostly innocent man victimized by circumstance. Indeed, Brown is so adamant on the matter of absolutely no arms negotiations that he at once tries to justify the tone of his preemptory response by explaining that the guns his men are holding along with a "few more breechloaders on board" represent their only marketable assets, and he plans "to sell the lot in Madagascar, if I ever get so far — begging my way from ship to ship" (p. 388). Jim, as imperceptive as ever, does not notice that this "explanation" regarding the necessary function of the weapons is compromised by the very circumstances in which it is uttered. Brown was hardly begging his way to Madagascar when he conducted his armed expedition upriver to Patusan.

Still another critic has more recently argued that Jim, in the matter of Brown and his weapons, "cannot fairly be considered even imprudent." As Watt admits in the same passage just quoted, "the catastrophe would not have occurred if Brown and his men had been disarmed." Nevertheless, he continues, "Jim had originally stipulated this and only yielded when Brown made it clear he would fight rather than surrender his arms."[30] And that is exactly the problem. If it is to be a fight, it is to be on Brown's terms. If it is to be a free road, it is also to be on Brown's terms. In short, the very evidence that Watt adduces to demonstrate Jim's prudence better illustrates his total obtuseness in dealing with Brown. We might notice, for example, how conveniently Brown's rationalization for keeping the weapons provides Jim with a better reason as to why they need not be kept any longer. The outlaw does not have to cross the Pacific before he can profit from his guns. According to his own testimony, what he really requires is supplies, and any cash he might obtain in Madagascar would have to be spent to provision his ship. So an exchange beneficial to both parties could be immediately arranged. Guns could be bartered for goods. Brown would not depart as a beggar dependent on chance encounters with ships possibly commanded by generous officers, while Jim could be considerably more certain that he had done right in releasing him and could also confidently anticipate that no one, particularly no inhabitants of Patusan, need suffer if Brown was not what he claimed to be. Conversely, a refusal to submit to the minor muzzling that trading away his guns might entail would clearly indicate that the outlaw leader's whole story was self-serving pretense, nothing more than a rat's attempt to escape from a trap.

Jim's first failures were prompted by an overactive imagination. On board the training ship, he did not "man the cutter" in time because he felt that the "brutal tumult of earth and sky" consciously intended his extermination (p. 7). In much the same fashion, his leap from the *Patna* was substantially motivated, as Marlow observed, by "his confounded imagination," which "had evoked for him all the horrors of panic, . . . all the appalling incidents of a disaster at sea" (p. 88). As Zdzislaw Najder observes, "in *Lord Jim* imagination is shown as a dangerous faculty, debilitating and destructive."[31] But Jim's truly disastrous misjudging of Brown is almost the converse of his earlier imagination-prompted lapses from what he believed was his duty. He finally quells all intimations about any possible tragedy and insists on assuming that the unperturbing surface of a situation (what he thinks he sees) represents its full reality, a "certitude" he earlier displayed on the *Patna* before the collision took place (p. 17). Instead of being undone by an overactive imagination, Jim, at the end of his career, suffers from an underactive one. He will not perceive in Brown possibilities other than those Brown himself duplicitously claims.

Marlow never criticizes Jim for his failure of vision. Conrad, however, makes it quite clear that the Bugis were not similarly short-sighted. For example, soon after he returned from the crucial encounter, Jim was assailed, Marlow writes, by an old woman "enjoining him in a scolding voice to see to it that her two sons, who were with Doramin, did not come to harm at the hands of the robbers." She responded to the laughter her clamor elicited with a stately, "What is this, O Muslims? This laughter is unseemly. Are they not cruel, bloodthirsty robbers bent on killing?" Jim then answered her with the promise, "Everybody shall be safe" (p. 391). She was right and he was wrong. And how ironic that an elderly native lady reads Brown better than does Jim, the outlaw's fellow white man. Or consider Doramin's reluctant assent to Jim's plea that they "let [the white men] go because this is best in my knowledge which has never deceived you." The old chief "raised his heavy head and said that there was no more reading of hearts than touching the sky with the hand, but — he consented" (p. 393). Doramin here dismisses Jim's claim that he spoke to the Bugis chief "before all the others, and alone, for you know my heart as well as I know yours and its greatest desire" (p. 389). The Bugis chief does not agree with Jim's counsel but he will let him have his way, while Jim ignores Doramin's wise advice about the impossibility of "reading" another's "heart" to insist that he fully comprehends Brown's. "But Jim did not know the almost inconceivable egotism of the man which made him, when resisted and foiled in his will, mad with the indignant and revengeful rage of a thwarted autocrat'' (p. 394). In short, one egotist egotistically refuses to recognize the egotism of another.

Almost all of the Bugis disagree with Jim's opinion that these ''erring men whom suffering had made blind to right and wrong'' (p. 391) are not fully responsible for their previous actions and deserve another chance. To provide them with that chance, Jim ''had for the first time to affirm his will in the face of out-spoken opposition'' (p. 391). But Marlow never examines how much that affirmation proclaims just where Jim stands. To start with, he does not simply offer his advice and then allow the assembled council to reach some basic consensus. Instead, Jim offers two problematic promises designed to impel the Bugis to accede to his proposed course of action. The first of these is a pledge which attests to his certainty that he is right: ''He was ready to answer with his life for any harm that should come to them if the white men with beards were allowed to retire'' (p. 392). A similar promise, it should be remembered, was given earlier. To convince the Bugis that they could overcome Sherif Ali, Jim ''had made himself responsible for success on his own head'' (p. 263). It might also be noted that the connection between Brown and Sherif Ali has already been suggested in the novel. As Tamb' Itam anticipated the possibility that the white invaders would be attacked, he asked, ''What was it but the taking of another hill?'' (p. 390). Thus Conrad doubly equates two impending battles but does so to emphasize the fact that, in these two roughly parallel situations, his protagonist has totally different reasons for making essentially the same promise. Jim first wagered his life as part of a plan to save Patusan from those who threatened it. When he pledges his head again, he would save those who threaten Patusan from its justly angered inhabitants.

Jim will doubly jeopardize himself to lead his people against Sherif Ali. But he will not put his life on the line in any battle with Brown and his men. If the Bugis decide to fight, then Dain Waris must command them, for, proclaimed Jim, ''in this business I shall not lead'' (p. 392). This second statement contradicts, even more than did the first one, the rhetorical flourish that preceded them both. Jim had ''declared to his hearers, the assembled heads of the people, that their welfare was his welfare, their losses his losses, their mourning his mourning'' (p. 392). However, by insisting that his advice must overrule the wishes of all others in Patusan, he immediately went on to demonstrate that their interests were not his interests. What one recent critic has termed ''his magnificent fidelity to the natives of Patusan'' is clearly compromised.[32]

Marlow's account of Jim's unfortunate victory over the better judgment of his adopted people is, itself, almost as morally questionable as the action described. For Marlow, Jim's final tragedy begins with ''the moment the sheer truthfulness of his last three years of life carries the day against the ignorance, the fear, and the anger of men" (p. 393). Yet it seems clear that the one who is acting most out of ignorance (and perhaps fear too) was Jim himself. Subsequent events certainly prove that those general "men" whom Marlow so condescendingly passes over, the natives at the council, were, with respect to Brown, wiser than their white lord. Their anger was a more appropriate response than his untested trust. Unfortunately, the Bugis also tended, but with considerably better reason than Jim, to misplace their confidence. The natives honored their white leader more than they hated Brown. When the former finished his speech, "most of them simply said that they 'believed Tuan Jim' " (p. 393).

"In this simple form of assent to his will," Marlow continues, "lies the whole gist of the situation; their creed, his truth; and the testimony to that faithfulness which made him in his own eyes the equal of the impeccable men who never fall out of the ranks" (p. 393). More, however, is at issue than Marlow admits. For one thing, Jim's "truth" cannot be, at the end of his career, so readily assumed. And neither can his "faithfulness" be simply posited. Faithful to what or to whom? Earlier, the answer might have seemed complimentary to Jim. At one time he did effectively aid Doramin and his people and thereby partly compensated for earlier abandoning other natives, the passenbers on the *Patna*, to what he at the time believed would be certain death. But after encountering Brown and hearing in that renegade's "rough talk a vein of subtle reference to their common blood, an assumption of common experience; a sickening suggestion of common guilt, of secret knowledge that was like a bond of their minds and of their hearts" (p. 387), it almost seems as if Jim has transformed his allegiance from the Bugis to Brown and the other white invaders of Patusan.

But I would argue that the encounter with Brown demonstrates the way Jim, all along, has had only one loyalty. He has been, persistently, true to his own egotism or, more specifically, to his increasingly desperate attempt to salvage his concept of himself as a potential hero. Furthermore, he has never been faithful in the sense Marlow implies, totally dedicated to serving the best interests of the Bugis and thus deserving their trust. Instead of redeeming himself, to quote Jackson Heimer, "he merely rehabilitates," on a very local level, his "good name."[33] Marlow is therefore especially mistaken when he maintains that Jim's "faithfulness . . . made him in his own eyes" as good as those who had never slipped. If Jim had adequately compensated for previous failings, he should better see himself for what he was and see Brown in the same way. It is precisely because Jim has not fully atoned in his own eyes for his earlier failures that he allows Brown to impose on him a rhetoric of their common sinfulness. The perceptive outlaw mocks the self-produced play in which Jim masquerades as a proven hero. And since it all is a masquerade, yet one that Jim insists on believing, he is so intent on reestablishing the role he believes he must play that he readily overlooks, as I have previously argued, how much the role he actually plays is directed by Brown and how totally that role subverts the one Jim thinks he acts.

Jim carries this self-deception even further. He tells Jewel that he will not rest until after Brown and company have departed, because "something might happen for which he would never forgive himself." Such comments prompt the girl to ask, "Are they very bad?" "After some hesitation," Jim answers, "Men act badly sometimes without being much worse than others" (p. 394). As Heimer observes, this estimation of the invaders is really the judgment Jim would have others make of him. He "is lenient with Brown because he wants leniency for himself."[34] Therefore, and contrary to what William Cook argues, Jim's "trust in Brown" is not simply another indication "that Jim cannot see things as they are in reality" and of a confidence based only "upon his own hazy ideal of the nobility of man."[35] Jim himself can well suspect that that ideal is rather hazy. He knows that he and Brown can act badly; he knows that they have both done so in the past; and, as much because of that knowledge as in spite of it, he still insists on assuming that Brown will justify his trust, even though the act of trusting the outlaw requires, as previously noted, that Jim betray the natives who have trusted him.

Jim's response to Jewel's question is significant in still another way. His final assessment of Brown clearly implies that, for Jim, existence is not essence, a consideration overlooked by those who would see this character as Conrad's existential man forging his own destiny in a senseless universe. Alvin Greenberg, for example, posits a Sisyphus-like "absurd hero" who, "over and over again," chooses life; who engages, with "painful dedication," in "the struggle for self"; and who finally "becomes 'stronger than his rock'."[36] Or, in an essay titled "Sartre and Conrad: Lord Jim as Existential Hero," Ira Sadoff suggests that Jim "is one of us" because "he has determined his own fate, he has learned to accept himself among men."[37] However, as Bruce Johnson astutely observes, "Jim . . . believes he has an ordained identity as hero, a predetermined self which, though experience may temporarily frustrate its appearance, will ultimately shine forth." And "to pursue the ideal as one's already innate essence is not to *pursue* it at all."[38] Or Said equally perceptively sees "the pressure on Jim that makes him favor death over life" as "a fatalistic desire to behold the self passively as an object told about, mused on, puzzled over, marvelled at fully, in utterance."[39] In either case — privileging essence or utterance — the result is the same: existentialism in bad faith. We see Jim dubiously dissociate what he "does" from what he "is" and then further confuse both sides of that division by how he "talks" about it. Marlow, moreover, earlier suspected as much. "Still the idea obtrudes itself that he made so much of his disgrace while it is the guilt alone that matters" (p. 177).

But Jim does not fully believe in the dichotomy of "is" and "does" (or disgrace and guilt) either. If a few slips do not particularly matter, then Jim should have no real need to try to redeem himself after one failure on the *Patna*. Obviously, deeds matter. Yet, in another context, actual actions do not count for much after all. Jim's crucial failure on the *Patna* is not cancelled out by his subsequent success in Patusan. And just as that success brought him the test of Brown, it also almost assures his defeat in that test by the very fact that no prior success can be successful enough. In short, Jim cannot completely trust his own reclaimed virtue and so necessarily advocates a philosophy of second chances.

Given that second chance, Brown shows what he can do. He makes a surprise attack on Dain Waris and the other natives guarding the river. Told of that "act of cold-blooded ferocity" (p. 403), Jim first decides to pursue and punish the offenders. That plan proves short-lived. Tamb' Itam, who brought the news of the massacre, hesitantly informs his master that the "orders to assemble a fleet of boats for immediate pursuit" cannot be executed: "It is not safe for thy servant to go out amongst the people" (p. 408). "Then Jim understood." Marlow immediately continues: "He had retreated from one world, for a small matter of an impulsive jump, and now the other, the work of his own hands, had fallen in ruins upon his head" (p. 408). That passive "had fallen" typifies the various techniques whereby Marlow attempts to minimize the degree to which Jim is responsible for his own defeat. In the formulation that soon follows we see even more clearly an attempt to wrest out of Jim's reaction to his defeat some victory for the defeated man. "I believe that in that very moment he had decided to defy the disaster in the only way it occurred to him such a disaster could be defied" (pp. 408-9). We have here Marlow's postulation of Jim's motive ("I believe") as a credo defining Jim's final act. Choosing death *is* defying fate. On that strained equation the whole conclusion of the novel turns.[40] "The dark powers should not rob him twice of his peace" (p. 409). Nor his honor either, if Marlow has anything to say in the matter.

The narrator regularly tries to see Jim's final act as almost heroic. "There was nothing to fight for. He was going to prove his power in another way and conquer the fatal destiny itself" (p. 410). But Marlow's first description of this decision suggests that it was prompted primarily by Jim's egotism, by a selfish concern for his "peace" regardless of the cost to others. Furthermore, Jim's suicide becomes even more dubious when assessed in the context of the whole novel and thereby contrasted to another suicide which Marlow earlier, and rather critically, described. As Cheris Kramer observes: "[Jim] kills himself, in effect, because, like Brierly, he cannot live with his self-consciousness. Brierly cannot bear to live with the idea of his own flaws or with the possibility that he might duplicate Jim's failure; Jim cannot bear to live with his new self-knowledge or with the thought that he might yet again fail at a moment of crisis."[41]

Brierly, however, sheds his burden of self-consciousness with much more responsibility than does Jim.

Admittedly, Jim had "guaranteed one kind of legitimacy for his suicide by earlier pledging his life should anything go wrong in the release of Gentleman Brown."[42] But that "legitimacy" is itself fundamentally illegitimate. The pledge was one that should never have been offered, that could (and did) require Jim to betray earlier vows that should have been more binding. Jim, of course, ignores the existence of all previous commitments — what Marlow is still dubiously calling "the truth that surely lived in his heart" (p. 409) — when he decides to abandon Patusan and its people, particularly Jewel and Tamb' Itam, to whatever fate might befall them. Reminded of one explicit promise, "Do you remember you said you would never leave me? ... You promised unasked — remember," he simply brushes the promise and the promised aside: "Enough poor girl, . . . I should not be worth having" (p. 412). Ignoring Jewel's counsel to "fight" or "fly," he insists he will do neither. He goes to his death, as Jewel, understandably, cries after him that he is "false" and that she will "never" forgive him (p. 414).

Realizing his own position on Patusan when told that his personal servant's life is in danger, Jim decides on death, leaving Tamb' Itam to save himself as best he can and abandoning Jewel to the fate she most feared. Brierly, however, did all he could to assure that none of his subordinates or dependents would come to harm and even recommended that his generally antagonistic mate be appointed his successor. The captain of the *Ossa* took special measures to chart the safest possible course for his vessel, while the former mate of the *Patna* simply abandons Patusan and its inhabitants much as he abandoned his ship and its passengers. Brierly actually showed more concern for his gold chronometer, one token of previous heroism — "he had saved lives at sea, had rescued ships in distress" (p. 57) — than Jim shows for Patusan, the proof of his heroism and not a token at all but the triumph itself, the one thing he could claim he had helped to save. More telling still is the way in which Brierly arranges for the safety of even his dog, shutting it up so that it could not "jump after him" (p. 61), as compared to Jim's complete indifference about what might happen to Jewel. As Jacques Berthoud observes in another context, "even at a moment of supreme irresponsibility, [Brierly] remains the model of the responsible officer."[43] And Jim, at another moment of supreme irresponsibility, remains the model of the irresponsible officer. The one schooled in discipline, the other schooled in dreams, neither really changes although each ends much the same.

"Who can tell what flattering view he had induced himself to take of his own suicide?" (p. 64). Thus Marlow assessed Captain Brierly's self-inflicted death, but, as David Daiches briefly notes, "the question could even more appropriately be asked of Jim, whose final death is really a form of suicide."[44]

Marlow, however, looks critically at only the first case, not at the second. He can discern in the aftermath of Brierly's death an "inexpressibly mean pathos" and "the posthumous revenge of fate" (p. 64), while Jim, perhaps, "at the last . . . confessed to a faith mightier than the laws of order and progress" (p. 339). Indeed, Marlow at the end tends to evaluate Jim's death as generously as Jim himself might, and formulations such as "conquer the fatal destiny itself" could well derive from either of the two. Yet the early condemnation of one self-inflicted death must subvert in advance the narrator's subsequent attempt to valorize another. Again we see that the voice of the narration and the views of the author are not necessarily in complete accord. More simply put, Conrad's structuring of the whole text contradicts Marlow's asserted reading of its conclusion.

Another crucial contrast also calls Marlow's assessment of Jim's death into question. It will be noted that certain details in Marlow's account of that last act link it with his earlier description of "the greatest active success in Jim's life, in fact almost his only active success," the storming of Sherif Ali's hilltop fort. As Guerard also observes, the earlier "portrait of Doramin . . . carried up the hill in his armchair . . . with a pair of flintlock pistols on his knees" functions "above all" as a means of preparing us to recognize and believe the Doramin of the last pages and those pistols on his knees: the deliberateness of the shooting, and the ironic closing of a circle as the ring rolls against Jim's foot."[45] Jim's end is thus the obverse of his earlier success and not the culmination of it.

The ironic circle that Guerard persuasively delineates is not the only one closed at the novel's conclusion. The ring was, for Jim, originally a romantic talisman. It was "like something you read of in a book," and, as "a sort of credential," it was also a pledge that "Doramin would do his best for him" when he arrived in Patusan (pp. 233-34). But even as he told of a token "that would serve his turn immensely," Jim suddenly realized that he might have misplaced it: "The ring! The ring! Where the devil . . ." (p. 234). A suspected loss anticipates an actual one. "The talisman that had opened for him the door of fame, love, and success" is last seen lying, as if discarded, on the ground (p. 415). It was necessarily lost when Jim sent it with Tamb' Itam to Dain Waris. What "vouched for the truth of the messenger's words" that the invaders "were to be allowed to pass down the river" (p. 402) also attested to how carelessly Jim treated Brown. Because of that characteristic carelessness, Dain Waris — who was, Jim earlier told Marlow, "the best friend (barring you) I ever had" (p. 260) — is killed and Jim's position in Patusan is totally destroyed.

The ring, dropped from Doramin's hand at the end of the novel, suggests still another contrast and completes yet another circle. That token, it should be remembered, was originally given to Stein by Doramin when the German trader and the chief of the Bugis "parted for the last time" (p. 233). "Mr. Stein had been the means of saving that chap's life on some occasion; purely by accident, Mr. Stein had said, but he — Jim — had his own opinion about that. Mr. Stein was just the man to look out for such accidents" (p. 234). Thus Jim " ran on" (p. 233) about the "magnificent chance" (p. 241) he was being given, and, by extension, his own words later damn him. Lord Jim did not look out for accidents. Stein could rescue his friend just as he could also preserve his own life. "This wants a little management," he once observed to himself, when ambushed by "only seven . . . rascals" (pp. 209-10). Yet Jim, with Brown in his power, could not manage at all. The comparison is inescapable.[46] Stein saves himself and his "war-comrade." Jim saves neither. Instead, he causes the death of Dain Waris and then is himself shot with one of the dueling pistols which were, like the ring, a token of the relationship that had existed between one of Jim's figurative fathers and Dain Waris's real one.

The pistols, too, fit the same pattern and point the same way. Jim earlier described to Marlow those "magnificent" weapons that Doramin brought with him during the attack on Sherif Ali. They were "ebony, silver-mounted, with beautiful locks and a calibre like an old blunderbuss. A present from Stein, it seems — in exchange for that ring, you know. Used to belong to good old M'Neil" (p. 264). So the gift that partly attests to the earlier friendship between Stein and Doramin attests also to a still earlier one. M'Neil, moreover, had helped Stein when he first came to the East, and, as Marlow recognizes, Stein was "passing on to a young man the help he had received in his own young days" (pp. 230-31). From the first, he intends to make Jim his Patusan heir, just as the old Scotch trader had made Stein his Celebes heir. As Watt observes: "The continuity of this cycle of trust and friendship is broken." But it is not broken just when "Doramin avenges the death of his only son ... with the gift his old friend had given him to seal their friendship."[47] The responsibilities of friendship had passed down through several generations in reciprocal obligations — gifts and actions. To sustain that cycle required an awareness and capability that Jim clearly lacked. But Jim, breaking one circle, completes another, for he fails Stein just as he earlier failed other father figures such as Marlow or Mr. Denver. Although Jim initially seeks the understanding and approval of these substitute fathers, he still "deserts them [all] as he continues his quest for personal honor."[48]

Mr. Denver, as the tone of his second letter indicated, resented Jim's failure. Stein apparently does; Marlow, in the last sentences of the novel, notes how this former patron, who also picked up the pieces that remained after Jim was shot by Doramin, "has aged greatly of late" and is readying himself for death (pp. 416-17). Yet Marlow, to the very end, tries to find some triumph in the final action of the young man who was his protégé too. "They say that the white man sent right and left at all those faces [of the assembled natives] a proud and unflinching glance. Then with his hand over his lips he fell forward, dead." "And that's the end," the next paragraph begins. "He passes away under a cloud, inscrutable at heart, forgotten, unforgiven, and excessively romantic" (p. 416).

Not very promising material from which to wrest some victory. Marlow is nevertheless, as the immediately subsequent sentences attest, undeterred: "Not in the wildest days of his boyhood visions could he have seen the alluring shape of such an extraordinary success! For it may very well be that in the short moment of his last proud and unflinching glance, he had beheld the face of that opportunity which, like an Eastern bride, had come veiled to his side." Continuing the marriage metaphor, Marlow now sees Jim as a man who went "away from a living woman to celebrate his pitiless wedding with a shadowy ideal of conduct." And it is indeed a "shadowy ideal" that can transform one so recently simply "forgotten" into "an obscure conqueror of fame" (p. 416). The veil that masks Jim's final destiny, a veil several times alluded to earlier in the novel, is not really lifted at the end. Marlow, I would suggest, merely pretends that he might have done so.

The language Marlow here uses suggests the lineaments of a face he does not want to see. He wishes to claim at least partial success with Jim, to find him, in some saving way, "as genuine as a new sovereign" and not "nothing more rare than brass" (pp. 45-46). Thus the Jim we finally encounter, the "obscure conqueror of fame," the destiny behind a veil. But there are other contradicitons here besides the oxymoronic obscure fame. Marlow's posited destiny — opportunity like an Eastern bride, marriage to a shadowy ideal — implies more than the apologist intends. These marriage tropes must remind us how unconditionally Jim had pledged himself to Jewel. He already has his Eastern bride. Any second one must therefore represent a bigamous union, which hardly proves faithfulness. The one pledge Jim keeps also requires him to betray earlier vows that should have been more binding. He leaves the "living woman," whom we see again, in the last paragraph of the novel, "leading a sort of soundless inert life," to embrace, "at the call of his exalted egotism . . . a shadowy ideal of conduct." More accurately, Jim is still betraying those who depend on him and doing so because his "eternal constancy," which Marlow admits he "stood up once . . . to answer for" (p. 416), represents Jim's dedication only to his own exalted image of himself.

The same point is suggested another way in the concluding paragraphs of the novel. Marlow finds much of his evidence for Jim's heroism in the latter's "last proud and unflinching glance." As Tanner tellingly observes, the repetition at the conclusion of the book of the word *unflinching* should suggest the way in which the same word was used at the beginning of the novel.[49] The omniscient narrator there describes Jim's condition just before he fails his first test: he dreams that he can rise to any challenge; can be "always an example of devotion to duty, and as *unflinching* as a hero in a book" (p. 6, emphasis added). Even then Jim was assiduously preparing for his future. His destiny, simply put, was to remain Jim. Marlow, moreover, suspects as much. He cannot really believe in the picture he paints (no more than Jim could believe in the role he acted). The narrator's last questions subvert his final account of Jim's death as much as that second narration subverts the first one that ostensibly centers on Jim's redemption. "Was I so very wrong after all?" Marlow asks, to answer with only another question: "Who knows?" (p. 416). Jewel knows. Conrad knows. Considering their answers, implicit and explicit in the novel, we, as readers and critics, can hardly indulge our taste for heroes and find in Jim some redeeming greatness.[50] That character, as Jim, an all too human victim of all too human weakness, can merit our sympathy, but as a lord he was always a sham.

This interpretation of his death deprives Jim of the personal glory and public acclaim that he dreamed so diligently of achieving but it does not necessarily consign him to unmitigated defeat and deserved obscurity. If, as a hero, Jim is definitely a failure, there is still something heroic in that failure. And again the patterns in the text come in to play. Compared to such human disasters as Chester, Captain Robinson, or the other officers on the *Patna*, Jim is most impressive indeed. Furthermore, although Brown's actions in their very effectiveness mock Jim's incompetence, Jim's intentions are still definitely preferable to those of the outlaw leader. In short, having disposed of Jim, the failed hero, we have not at all disposed of Jim, the heroic failure who went even into death trailing after intimations of immortality. The reader's problem is at the end, then, the same as Marlow's was at the beginning. What does one make of the unconscious duplicity and inescapable duality that inform Jim's most characteristic actions, which are, after all, dreams of imagined success and denials of real failure? We might also notice, in this respect, how much Jim's responses to his *Patna* and his Patusan defeats mirror each other as reversals in which nothing really is changed. At the naval Board of Inquiry Jim physically makes an accounting (refusing to slip away like the other officers), but at one and the same time he emotionally flees (with his self-justifying rationalizations and his assertions that anyone else — even Marlow — would have done just as he did) from the trial. At what we might call the Bugis Board of Inquiry Jim emotionally makes an accounting (overaccepting his guilt as a way of shedding his responsibility), but at one and the same time he physically flees (through seeking certain death) the trial.

The contradition at the heart of Jim is also, as Raval has recently emphasized, "a contradiction at the heart of Marlow's narrative."[51] Marlow, it will be remembered, wanted to believe in "the sovereign power enthroned in a fixed standard of conduct" and early in his first narration suspected that "the secret motive" for his "prying" was "to find some shadow of an excuse for that young fellow" so that he might lay his own "obstinate ghost" of "uneasy doubt" (pp. 50-51). He attempts, as previously noted, to see Jim in a favorable light and does so, more and more unconvincingly, until the very end of the novel. But despite his effort to redeem Jim, "Marlow's epistemological quest culminates ... with the disconfirmation of his belief that only a 'few simple notions' are required to meet the world outside oneself."[52] Yet the ideals still remain, denied and affirmed. "The narrative of *Lord Jim* . . . discloses the necessity of ideals for the effective functioning of the community, but it at the same time discloses the ideals as possessing an inhuman and absolute status in human life." What is "necessary for life in one context" is "inhuman and destructive in another." Furthermore, "each context implicitly leads to the other and neither is unquestionable."[53]

So Marlow's duplicitous narrative itself reflects a still larger duplicity, the "inauthenticity of human life as it is ordinarily lived" and "the fundamental inadequacy of all modes of (human) being."[54] Conrad also suggests that Marlow (even more admirable in his defeats than Jim is in his) comes to at least some realization of the impasses he confronts. In his letter to the privileged man (which he probably wrote after he had finished the second narration and which therefore well might be his last words on his different accounts of Jim and his deeds), Marlow remembers that, earlier, as he was leaving Patusan, Jim shouted after him a message to the outside world. "Tell them!" he began, but after a pause concluded with an inclusive, "No. Nothing." Marlow continues: "That was all then — and there shall be nothing more; there shall be no message, unless such as each of us can interpret for himself from the language of facts, that are so often more enigmatic than the craftiest arrangement of words" (pp. 339-40). Marlow, the privileged man, and the reader of the text, all face the problem of defining Jim, of deciding what his last message might be. Jim thereby becomes, as a kind of projection test, "one of us" in ways not originally anticipated and in ways that do not particularly illuminate the nature of Jim.[55] No last message, no clear meaning. Even the "language of facts" is, Marlow insisted, at least as problematically "enigmatic" as the "craftiest arrangement of words," for how else do the facts exist but as they are craftily expressed. Yet — and here is still a larger duplicity — words and deeds are finally incommensurate with one another. Marlow's different narrations can circumambulate Jim's experience but cannot capture it. Also, as the ending especially indicates, Jim and Marlow come to their conclusions in quite different fashions, life running out in one way and language in another. Nevertheless, these different closings are still conjoined and the unfinality of Marlow's ending somehow undoes the finality of Jim's. As Miller has observed, "the 'ending' of *Lord Jim* is Marlow's realization that it is impossible to write 'The End' to any story."[56]

2

Patterns in *Nostromo*

The conclusion of *Nostromo* is, at once, both more simple and more subtle than that of *Lord Jim*. Indeed, on one level, the later work seems to exhibit the closed ending eschewed in the earlier, for it terminates only after the social consequences of the silver mine have been substantially assessed, after Conrad fully portrays the public face of the "material interests" so often referred to in *Nostromo*. Different dreams of unlimited wealth, revolutions and counter-revolutions which are really no more than blatant attempts to obtain or retain the corrupting economic power inherent in the "incorruptible" silver, finally destroy the old state of Costaguana. Moreover, just as the treasure torn from a mountain necessarily entails the political vicissitudes that soon — historically speaking — sunder a country, so too does it occasion the schemes and counterschemes that lead most of the main characters in the novel to their various failures and defeats.

One of the more perceptive of these victims finally delineates for another the essential nature of the force that will continue to victimize them all. "There is no peace and no rest in the development of material interests. They have their law, and their justice. But it is founded on expediency, and is inhuman; it is without rectitude, without the continuity and the force that can be found only in a moral principle. Mrs. Gould, the time approaches when all that the Gould Concession stands for shall weigh as heavily upon the people as the barbarism, cruelty, and misrule of a few years back."[1] As H. M. Daleski dryly observes: "There is nothing in the novel to offset the doctor's prognostication."[2] And Mrs. Gould herself soon sees that she must concur with Dr. Monygham's condemning prophecy. "She saw the San Tomé mountain hanging over the Campo, over the whole land, feared, hated, wealthy; more soulless than any tyrant, more pitiless and autocratic than the worst government; ready to crush innumerable lives in the expansion of its greatness" (p. 251).

These explicit evaluations do not, however, completely resolve a central problem examined throughout the novel. Charles Gould early insisted: "I pin my faith to material interests. Only let the material interests once get a firm footing, and they are bound to impose the conditions on which alone they can continue to exist . . . . A better justice will come afterwards'' (p. 84). Thus the silver mine shall become a ''ray of hope,'' the ''little rift in the darkness'' of Costaguanian politics that his ''poor father despaired of ever seeing'' (p. 84). Yet this version of Holroyd's ''religion of silver and iron'' (p. 71) is almost as obviously self-serving as is its prototype, for it justifies ''the last of the Costaguana Goulds'' (p. 522) being totally preoccupied with his mine and is an early example of how Gould ''cannot act or exist [as Martin Decoud tellingly observed] without idealizing every simple feeling, desire, or achievement'' (pp. 214-15).

One is tempted to agree with Decoud's skeptical pronouncement on the nature of belief: ''What is a conviction? A particular view of our personal advantage either practical or emotional'' (p. 189). But Conrad also suggests that Decoud's early assessment of Gould as a man who insists on making his ''motives'' conform to ''some fairy tale'' (p. 215) is not self-evidently valid. One part of the denouement and the only comic episode in the concluding chapters of *Nostromo* implies that material interests might have, if not the power for good attributed to them by the owner of the silver mine, at least some redeeming features. I refer, of course, to Captain Mitchell's celebration of the progress that wealth has bought for the new Occidental Republic.

The subtle authorial humor inherent in the Captain's retrospective account of the success of the most recent revolution effectively serves several purposes and merits brief analysis. For example, Conrad begins by noting that this narrator adherred to a ''more or less stereotyped relation of the 'historical Events' which for the next few years was at the service of distinguished strangers visiting Sulaco'' (p. 473). Identical details, identical phrases even, came always in the same order. So Captain Mitchell, perpetually repeating his formulaic description of the latest Sulaco revolution, suggests something of the cyclical nature of Costaguanan reality.

The Captain's story also implies another aspect of life, especially political life, in one particular South American republic. The narrator presumably has many of his facts right but he is not particularly adept at communicating them and thus burdens any ''privileged passenger'' of the Oceanic Steam Navigation Company with disparate bits of information which the recipient cannot possibly comprehend. This put-upon auditor is an obvious stand-in for the reader, who is also, in a different sense, a guest of the nation, and, as such, is forced to confront much that is senseless and chaotic. But the reader, especially towards the end of the novel, need not be perplexed in the same fashion as is Mitchell's hapless tour victim. Indeed, one immediate artistic function of the Captain's disconnected account is to provide items of information — such as Pedrito the Guerillero's briefly noted final fate, ''keeping a disorderly house in one of the southern ports'' (p. 487) — the appropriateness of which the reader at least can fully comprehend.

The comic confusion in Captain Mitchell's narration serves, however, a still more basic purpose. It soon becomes evident that that narrator himself is almost as hopelessly at sea as is the unlucky guest to whom he shows the city and surrounding countryside. This self-appointed guide's obtuseness is especially suggested by the manner in which his recitation winds to its close. He has emphasized, egotistically, how much *his* Capataz de Cargadores did for Sulaco; has observed, erroneously, how little Nostromo received in return.[3] Then, to be sure that his listener does not escape the possible benefit of any facts perhaps previously overlooked, he passes disconnectedly from the coasting schooner with which the savior of Sulaco was finally officially rewarded to the much earlier interview between Nostromo and Miss Avellanos. He tells of how "poor Doña Antonia," informed of her fiancé's death, "burst into tears when [Nostromo] told her how Decoud had happened to say that his plan would be a glorious success" (p. 489). Only then does Captain Mitchell recall that Martin Decoud also played a substantial role in establishing Sulaco. On that note the whole narration about the manner in which the Occidental Republic came into being winds to its close: "And there's no doubt, sir, that it is. It is a success" (p. 489).

As William Bonney observes, Captain Mitchell fully accepts a statement that Decoud himself never believed. But Bonney overstates his case when he claims that "Nostromo lied in conveying such a message to Decoud's 'intended'."[4] Decoud did ask that Antonia be told he was "looking forward to a glorious and successful ending of my mission" (p. 300). These words were, admittedly, expressed with a "touch of contempt for himself," an "ironic tone" that "Nostromo detected" (pp. 300-1). Nostromo is, therefore, less than candid but not completely dishonest when he is later called upon to tell Doña Antonia of all that transpired during the silver saving expedition. He will comfort the bereaved woman and protect himself and the hidden treasure by telling only partial truths. Captain Mitchell subsequently takes one detail in Nostromo's equivocal story and makes it his final word on the new Occidental Republic. Considering his dubious source and obvious obtuseness, Mitchell's very certainty suggests that his concluding declamation well might be questioned.[5]

Conrad soon provides another hint that Sulaco might not be such a great success. The Captain's victim, knowing nothing of Miss Avellanos's intended or of that gentelman's political machinations, forgets even "to ask himself, 'What on earth Decoud's plan could be?' " (p. 489). The listener here resembles his loquacious host who also has no real basis for posing questions as to what Decoud's intentions were and who cannot peer beyond the surface of things, the immediately flourishing Occidental Republic, to ask if and to what degree those plans proved successful. Entertaining none of the doubts that are later voiced by Dr. Monygham or Mrs. Gould, the Captain does not see that the new state rests on precisely the same uncertain foundation as did the old, the treasure of the San Tomé mine. Moreover, although he notes the role played by the United States in engineering "an international naval demonstration, which put an end to the Costaguana-Sulaco War" (p. 487), the elderly English sailor does not perceive that this is a service for which some return can be expected. Earlier, Holroyd, the North American capitalist, maintained that his country eventually will "be giving the word for everything" and thus shall "run the world's business whether the world likes it or not" (p. 77). At the end of the novel neither his company nor his country controls the world but they both certainly shall have a larger say in the affairs of the Occidental (the name is no accident) Republic.

Captain Mitchell's confusing tour terminates, then, with the implied question of whether or not Decoud achieved "success," "glorious" or otherwise. But no definitive answer can be immediately provided. If the country is less free than the Captain imagines, its future less secure, it has still at least temporarily escaped from the depredations of the Sotillos and the Pedritos, the tyrannies of the Guzman Bentos and the General Monteros who have previously produced, according to Don José Avellanos's too accurate title, "Fifty Years of Misrule." Hernandez the bandit, under the new order, becomes "the famous Hernandez, Minister of War" (p. 480), an improvement not only for Hernandez but also for travelers on the Campo. They too will profit from the former robber's rise in status, from his new, more honorable occupation. Yet is a bandit elevated to Minister of War really that different from a Minister of War who sees his official position as a license to steal? In each case, we see the same blurring of what should be a distinction between two quite different professions.

Decoud has succeeded. But nothing countermands Dr. Monygham's condemnation of the unfolding consequences of that success. "Politically, we follow the tumultous evolution of Sulacan society both to the cynical wisdom of Dr. Monygham's anti-progressivism and to the portentous platitudes of Captain Mitchell's imperialist faith."[6] And how does the reader resolve this contradiction? A solution can, perhaps, be found by assessing the book from another perspective, by considering not the state of the larger political entity as it is last portrayed, but the final fates of various characters who discover their own destinies within that macrocosm and thereby illustrate something of its nature.

No one's end is simpler, more stark than that of Señor Hirsch. The enterprising dealer in hides is first and finally a victim. "Maddened by apprehension" (p. 272) on shore, cowering terrified in the moored lighter that will immediately be used to remove "a whole six months' working" (p. 219) of silver, he is ruled by one "overpowering" passion, the desire to escape from a "terrible Sulaco" (p. 273). However, as Robert Haugh observes, even though

Hirsch "most vehemently wanted to avoid involvement," he could not do so, and "his brief action, ending in an imbecile death that was all a mistake, offers an object lesson in the bizarre potentialities of the revolution."[7] Hirsch dies, of course, because of the Monterist uprising. But tortured and killed by Sotillo, his fate implies something more than the fact that revolutions affect even — affect especially — the most insignificant of characters.

Hirsch is, essentially, killed by cupidity. His death can therefore illustrate something of the nature of that force. First, it is shown to have a power crudely proportionate to the desirability of the object coveted. Sotillo is intrigued by Captain Mitchell's chronometer but not to the point that he loses all sense of perspective on what he is doing. When his greed focuses on a shipload of silver, however, he becomes a victim of his own willed delusions and so, protractedly and much more brutally, does Señor Hirsch. The latter's suffering and death thus demonstrate not just the power of "material interests" but also the manner in which they govern the behavior of "property minded" men. Sotillo's blind belief that the silver cannot be irretrievably lost justifies, by the very force of that desire, any measures, including torture, necessary to obtain the missing treasure. The same delusion also underlies the frustrated rage which prompts him to shoot, senselessly, the one person who knows, he insists, where the treasure might have been hidden.

In brief, Sotillo, in his dealings with Hirsch, embodies a concept basic to the novel. The materialistic imagination is moved by the vision of what it might possess; the more it is moved, the more it forces the suppression of any rational promptings at odds with the dream. As the voice of the ironically aloof narrator observes, "There is no credulity so eager and blind as the credulity of covetousness" (p. 450). Sotillo perfectly exemplifies this maxim. While steaming into port after the collision with some smaller ship, he is, on one level, aware of what must have occurred. The other vessel had to have some reason for braving, at that particular time, the total darkness of the Golfo Placido. What is more probable than someone else then attempting to take away the treasure he knows he intends to seize? But "the idea that he had destroyed the principal object of his expedition was too intolerable to be accepted" (p. 294). Thus the theory that the silver must have been hidden, that Hirsch must know where, and the latter's torture and death.

The same solipsistic insistence that objective reality accord with his own desires later dooms Sotillo just as it earlier killed Hirsch. The commander of the Esmeralda regiment readily accepts Dr. Monygham's intentionally misleading story of silver sunk off shore to be recovered later by divers. Having no divers, Sotillo must drag the harbor. He is still dragging, desperate, "raving and foaming with disappointment," when "the first of Barrios's transports" arrives unnoticed and, "ranging close alongside," announces itself with devastating fire (p. 484). Sotillo did not read, in the demise of Señor Hirsch, his own fate which here overtakes him.

Sotillo, in short, is not so different from his victim as he would like to believe. It will be remembered that he works "himself up to the right pitch of ferocity" to torture Hirsch soon after he and his men are visited by Pedrito's impudently witty emissary (p. 446). That ambassador, addressed by an Esmeraldian officer who delivered "a panegyric upon Sotillo" that concluded with "an absurd colloquialism current amongst the lower class of Occidentals" — the claim that Colonel Sotillo was "a man of many teeth" — responded by claiming for his own commander a similar "catalogue of perfections," but with a comic — and ominous — addition: Pedrito is also "a dentist" (pp. 444-45). Then, almost immediately after this exchange, the pathetic Hirsch, subjected to the estrapade, "screamed with uplifted eyebrows and a wide-open mouth — incredibly wide, black, ominous, *full of teeth* — comical" (p. 447, italics added). But Sotillo does not heed the message coming out of that paradoxically ominous mouth.

The truth Hirsch expresses is metaphysical, not material; it can be voiced far more tellingly by a dead man than by a living one. Hanging rigid, at last at rest, the murdered hide merchant becomes "a sinister symbol of the fate that attends those who become involved with the silver and all it stands for."[8] Sotillo discovers this truth but never recognizes it, as, following Hirsch, he sacrifices himself and his men to the Mammon of "material interests."

If Hirsch's is the first significant death to take place towards the conclusion of the novel, Martin Decoud's is the second. But the sophisticated Costaguanero's suicide raises more perplexing problems than does the earlier senseless yet suggestive murder of the hide merchant. To start with, the journalist of Sulaco seems to possess some of his creator's basic tendencies and characteristics. Norman Sherry, for example, observes, "in Decoud Conrad drew close to presenting something of his own nature."[9] Irving Howe makes essentially the same suggestion: "If in Captain Mitchell Conrad gently scratched at one of his occasional masks, in Decoud he violently tore at one of his major attitudes."[10] Moreover, as Albert Guerard notes, the ironically aloof voice that narrates most of *Nostromo* "certainly shares" Decoud's "total cosmic skepticism."[11]

Yet this same character's perspective on himself and his society somehow merits explicit authorial condemnation. Almost as soon as he appears in the novel, he is described as "an idle young boulevardier" whose "cosmopolitanism" was "in reality a mere barren indifferentism posing as intellectual superiority" (p. 152). Furthermore, Decoud is not at all redeemed by his later social and political involvement, by his love for Antonia and the major role he plays in founding a new republic. He is finally shown to be, Joyce Carol Oates maintains, "just another character in Captain Mitchell's rambling history. And even Conrad turns against him — is not content with merely killing him off, but must pass judgment on his death, in the most wickedly dogmatic terms."[12] It seems, as Oates further suggests, that "the more [this] character approaches Conrad's own position, the more cruelly must he be repudiated."[13]

The reader is faced, then, with a fundamental question. Does Don Martin's final fate reflect mostly Conrad's idiosyncratic disapproval of a certain type of ethos and personality — his own — and thereby serve to illuminate not the meaning of the novel but the workings of its author's mind? Or does Decoud's silver-laden dive into the immensely somnolent Golfo Placido derive from his essential nature as well as his situation at the time of that act and does it relate to other themes and issues in *Nostromo*? In short, is the suicide integrated into the novel or authorially and arbitrarily imposed? Perhaps the best way to answer this question and to assess the significance of this particular episode in *Nostromo* is to pay particular attention to the etiology of the "brilliant son Decoud's" final self-defeat.

A close study of the way in which Decoud's last days are described suggests that his death well might relate to the manner in which another character was victimized by the silver. Decoud's "final attitude to the universe," C.B. Cox notes, "is expressed by an image of torture." When, in a solitude that " 'appeared like a great void,' " he " 'hung suspended by both hands' " from a " 'silence' " that seemed " 'a tense, thin cord,' " his "position recalls that of Señor Hirsch, undergoing the horror of the estrapade."[14] This same point was earlier made by Alan Friedman who also observed that Hirsch's "physical" and Decoud's "spiritual" suffering are similarly ended.[15] Martin Decoud, when he began to wish that the immaterial cord from which he metaphorically hangs might break, "imagined it snapping with the report as of a pistol — a sharp, full crack" (pp. 498-99). And soon he dies from a pistol shot, just as Hirsch had earlier done. There is, however, still another way in which the two deaths are similar. Each poses an enigma for Nostromo. Furthermore, although the most capable Capataz cannot read in the evidence that he encounters what finally happened to Hirsch or Decoud, he still senses that somehow he might share either's fate, a suspicion that eventually proves correct. He too is corrupted by the incorruptible silver and killed because he tried to master what had already mastered him. In more senses than one, all three men were in the same boat. Consequently, it is not surprising that Decoud's death is anticipated by Hirsch's (and Sotillo's); that these earlier deaths anticipate Nostromo's.

There is, however, another way in which Conrad incorporates the suicide into the larger design of the novel. A character's death generally attests to the basic nature of his life. Hirsch, for example, is first described as a pathetic victim. Coming to Sulaco, he encountered Nostromo on the road and, afraid that the other was a thief, "tried to hide behind a small bush" (p. 201). Later he is killed, and not just by Sotillo's greed. Hirsch's almost ludicrous fear also insures his death, for he is too much the helpless victim of his own terror to seize on any way to save himself. As Nostromo observes, "that terrified wretch . . . had no invention. None! none! Not like me. I could have told Sotillo a deadly tale for very little pain" (pp. 460-61).

Confronting death, Hirsch becomes even more what he always was — a victim destined to suffer. Decoud too becomes, in the course of the novel, the man he has always been and comes to recognize that fact. Furthermore, his final fate is also early foreshadowed. Determined to draw some response from Antonia, he emphasizes the danger inherent in his recently undertaken political activities. "With a sort of jocular desperation," he insists that if "you spend your time in inciting poor ignorant fools to kill and to die" the only end you can expect is to "go to the wall" (p. 181). This extended mocking assessment of his prospects is prompted primarily by his love for Antonia and is designed to elicit a concerned response. When he receives just such a response, her statement, " 'Martin, you will make me cry,' he remained silent for a minute, startled, as if overwhelmed by a sort of awed happiness, with the lines of the mocking smile still stiffening about his mouth, and incredulous surprise in his eyes" (p. 181). Yet the very behavior that prompts an indirect confession of love is also a betrayal of that love and thus anticipates a future betrayal much more serious than the present taunting, teasing comments. After his suicide, his "beloved" will have far greater occasion to weep. Decoud, moreover, in teasing the woman he loved, suggested that she seemed "satisfied to see my life hang on a thread" (p. 180). But it is, of course, he himself who here sees his life as precariously suspended, who later does so again, and who then breaks the cord from which he figuratively hangs.

"The brilliant Costaguanero of the boulevards," the narrator tells us, "died from solitude and want of faith in himself and others" (p. 496). But this explanation has not been accepted as definitive. Guerard, for example, argues that we really have in the novel "two Decouds": one who "fathers a revolution, yet all the while (through his lucid insight into men's motives) maintains intellectual integrity"; the other " immobilized in total physical isolation and in the exile of utter unbelief." For Guerard, it is this second character who kills himself. He finds it "hard to believe" that the first, "the active and loving Decoud," could "commit suicide so soon."[16] A more recent critic makes much the same argument: "If we consider all that he actually achieves in the novel Decoud's suicide does not appear warranted."[17] The crucial contradiction, however, might not be between what Decoud does and his subsequent suicide but between what he says as opposed to what he subsequently does. "There is nothing I would not do for the sake of Antonia" (p. 213), he insisted to Mrs. Gould. Similarly, writing to his sister, Don Martin asserted, "My dear girl, there is that in Antonia which would make me believe in the feasibility of anything." He claims that "she is more to me than his Church to Father Corbelan" or "his precious mine to that sentimental Englishman" (p. 238). Clearly, with respect to Antonia, he has "promises to keep." Yet his love for her is not enough, we soon see, to sustain, in isolation, his life for even two weeks. What then is the nature of his commitment to Antonia; what is his rationale for the role he plays in the politics of his country; and how do both relate to his last act, his doubly insured death?

Decoud himself emphasizes the relationship between his feelings for Miss Avellanos and his uncharacteristic political aspirations. He acknowledges to Antonia "that though she had managed to make a Blanco journalist of him, he was no patriot" (p. 186). And even more explicitly: "No one is a patriot for nothing. The word serves us well. But I am clear-sighted, and I shall not use that word to you, Antonia! I have no patriotic illusions. I have only the supreme illusion of a lover" (p. 189). It is as a lover, then, that he argues for succession and the political independence of Sulaco. As he admits to Mrs. Gould: "I cannot part with Antonia, therefore the one and indivisible Republic of Costaguana must be made to part with its western province. Fortunately, it happens to be also a sound policy. The richest, the most fertile part of this land may be saved from anarchy" (p. 215).

Decoud, first as a propagandizing journalist serving the Ribierest cause and then as the "apostle of Separation," does not at all believe in the intrinsic validity of the social objectives that he attempts to realize. Furthermore, he finds the means he must employ to achieve any political ends as dubious as those ends themselves. To "call Montero a *gran' bestia* every second day in the *Porvenir,"* he observes, can hardly be considered "a serious occupation" (p. 177). Indeed, for Decoud, "no occupation is serious" (p. 177), neither journalist nor liberator. Don Martin points out that even "the great Liberator Bolivar" himself finally admitted that "America is ungovernable" and that "those who worked for her independence have ploughed the sea" (p. 186). So only his love for Antonia persuades him to persist in activities that are, he suspects, both senseless and doubly deadly. "There is no room," he observes, for "some effective truth" in either "politics or journalism" (p. 177). Yet if he fails in either occupation he will be killed by the Monterists and even if he succeeds, by the very processes that brought about that success, he will have "killed [his] self-respect" (p. 180).

Decoud labors at public tasks he finds senseless to effect a political revolution in which he does not believe. He does so — and this is one of the chief ironies in *Nostromo* — for the sake of a love that finally proves equally unsubstantial. The crucial significance of his isolation on the island is to dramatize precisely that fact. Not at all committed to his fellow citizens, he soon ceases to see them as human beings. By the fifth day of his solitude, he had "resolved not to give himself up to these people in Sulaco, who had beset him, unreal and terrible, like jibbering and obscene spectres" (pp. 497-98). This reaction should not be particularly surprising; Decoud never had "given himself" to his fellow citizens. But Antonia, by the fifth day, is also becoming almost as dehumanized as those other "jibbering . . . spectres." The passage just quoted continues: "He saw himself struggling feebly in their [the other Costaguanerians] midst and Antonia, gigantic and lovely like an allegorical statue, looking on with scornful eyes at his weakness" (p. 498). Another five days and the woman he claimed he loved has been reduced to the same level of meaninglessness as everything else. The figurative "cord to which he hung with both hands vibrated with senseless phrases, always the same but utterly incomprehensible, about Nostromo, *Antonia,* Barios, and proclamations mingled into an ironical and senseless buzzing" (p. 499, italics added). Conrad thereby shows, with the very vibrating of this imagined cord from which Decoud figuratively hangs, that there is nothing to sustain him. He must plunge to his death in the blank immensity of the Golfo Placido.

And again Conrad early foreshadows a character's final fate. Decoud, we have seen, acts primarily because of his feelings for Antonia. But the discerning reader should note that the self-asserted love which this character insists both justifies his life (his rationale for political involvement) and shall sustain it (those "promises to keep") is, from the beginning, rather flimsy indeed. Even the actual phrases Decoud first uses to proclaim his feelings for Antonia suggest that the then asserted emotion might be differently interpreted: "I have only one aim in the world," he tells her, and it has been "always . . . in my heart — ever since the day when you snubbed me so horribly in Paris" (p. 179). But a skeptical reader might sense in the parenthetically noted genesis of the love that he here proclaims a second covert purpose. As Harry Marten observes, because she once criticized him, Decoud "can regain his sense of stature only by conquering Antonia's 'austere' personality."[18] Decoud never acknowledges such motivation, but then, as Decoud so regularly observes, all those around him never acknowledge their secret motivations either. In short, Conrad suggests that even with Decoud, the cynical denouncer of others' self-deception, the self deceives itself in the shadow of a different self that it pretends to be.

"By all the saints and devils I shall let the sea have the treasure rather than give it up to any stranger," Nostromo insisted to Decoud as they rowed on the dark gulf. "Since it was the good pleasure of the Caballeros to send me off on such an errand, they shall learn I am just the man they take me for" (p. 267). The wealth of the surrounding country, the expanse of the bordering campo, the backdrop of the sundering mountains, the vast placidity of the encroaching gulf all serve to make Sulaco, in William Bonney's apt term, "a narcissist's utopia." As Bonney observes: "Only ... such openness can receive the many significances imposed upon it."[19] Here is the self-dramatist's plenty, a realm in which fables of identity — whether the fabled identity be garnered from others or self-engendered — can be abundantly acted. Thus Nostromo will prove that he is the man they take him for, while Decoud shall demonstrate that he is the man he takes himself for, and both exercises in definition are essentially the same. What is reflected back in this mirror of land and sea is not the narcissist as hero but the hero as narcissist. And for the narcissist there is no escape. Thus the three men sailing out into the dark gulf and the darker night are seemingly voyaging to a new life, a new freedom, but they actually sail right back again and back to an even more implacable version of the very fate they fled.

This pattern is most simple and obvious with Hirsch. Terrified, he runs from danger; running, he rushes into the very torture and death from which he would escape. And just as his ordeal of the estrapade is a physical representation of the more metaphysical suffering that Decoud also for a time endures, so too is Hirsch's voyage a more objective version of a similar voyage made by Decoud. Both, in a sense, end where they began only more so. The hide merchant who feared unreasonably finds his worst fears realized. Decoud, posing as a skeptic who sees through all poses, finds even that pose sham. Consider, for example, Decoud's reaction when the ships collide: "The prospect of finding himself in the water and swimming, overwhelmed by ignorance and darkness, *probably in a circle,* till he sank from exhaustion was revolting." The "barren and cruel futility of such an end," the narrator notes, "intimidated his *affectation of careless pessimism*" (p. 282, italics added). His pessimism will soon become less affected; he will be, in earnest, the man he only pretended to be.

Decoud, who in Paris summed up his country's politics as "quelle farce!", nevertheless allows himself to be entangled in those same politics. He agrees to buy modern European arms for the President plotting against his own War Minister and then returns to Costaguana to see the rifles safely delivered and perhaps to buttress his contempt for the whole show by taking a closer look at the "comic business of stage statesmen, brigands, etc., etc.," whose "farcical stealing, intriguing, and stabbing is done in dead earnest," while "the blood flows all the time, and the actors believe themselves to be influencing the fate of the universe" (p. 152). But he soon plays in the comedy even if he does not fully believe in his role. Prompted by Antonia, Decoud becomes the "Journalist of Sulaco," then the "Apostle of Separation." Playing in the comedy, he also, when politics does not go as planned, has to flee, and when escape does not go as planned either, he finds himself isolated on the island. In that isolation, he is forced to recognize how fatuous his actions were, how he had worked to remake his world and so played a senseless part in what he had all along known was "une farce macabre." Moreover, he finally recognizes his motives, sees — at least figuratively — that he has acted out of an asserted but not a real love, and partly understands why.

For Hirsch, "the horror" was his cowardice, his fear of suffering. Decoud must face his own essential emptiness. When he decides "that Antonia could not possibly have ever loved a being so impalpable as himself" (p. 498), that is clearly not her judgment. He projects on others, almost to the end, an ultimately inescapable evaluation of himself, for others can be regularly proved wrong. But just as Hirsch achieves a minor victory over himself when he spits on Sotillo and thus precipitates the pistol shot that ends his suffering, so too does Decoud at last face the full implication of what he has all along professed to believe. Solitude and sleeplessness strip away his defenses, and he becomes a complete skeptic, skeptical about even his formerly protective skepticism. The consequence is his suicide but a suicide informed by still another implicit recognition. When Decoud takes four of the bars of silver to weight his dive into the Golfo Placido, he recognizes that the true power of wealth is the power of oblivion; that the silver is an agent of death and disappearing, not of being and becoming.

"It is done," Decoud "stammered out, in a sudden flow of blood," just after he shot himself and before he fell, as planned, from the boat (p. 501). But he becomes no Christ-figure, and no one is redeemed by his empty sacrifice of his own life. Nothing, in fact, is finished. Conrad immediately describes how, "after a few days, another form appeared striding away from the setting sun to sit motionless and awake in the narrow black gully all through the night in nearly the same pose, in the same place in which had sat that other sleepless man" (p. 501). This depersonalized "form" at first seems to be a returned reincarnation of Decoud who earlier rowed "straight towards the setting sun" (p. 500), but it is, we are soon told, "the magnificent Capataz de Cargadores" (p. 501) who has come back to the buried silver.

This implied equivalence of Nostromo and Decoud is proved by the subsequent text. Just as Decoud suffered a somewhat different version of Hirsch's tragedy, so too does Nostromo now proceed to reenact Decoud's to become thereby another reembodiment of that recently deceased man. This second parallel is, if anything, too obviously stressed. After swimming to the dinghy that "had come out to meet him empty and inexplicable," Nostromo, near the scene of Decoud's death, sitting in the boat, obsessed with the mystery of the other's disappearance, "resembled a drowned corpse come up from the bottom to idle away the sunset hour in a small boat" (p. 492). Reaching the island, he immediately passes "a night of sleeplessness as tormenting as any" endured by his former "companion in the most desperate affair of his life"; sleepless, "he wondered how Decoud had died" (pp. 501-02). That question has just been, for the reader, conclusively answered: "*A victim of the disillusioned weariness which is the retribution meted out to intellectual audacity,* the brilliant Don Martin Decoud, weighted by the bars of San Tomé silver, disappeared without a trace, swallowed up in the immense indifference of things" (p. 501, italics added). And as he ponders the fate of the dead man, Nostromo is portrayed, in strikingly similar language, as *"victim of the disenchanted vanity which is the reward of audacious action* (p. 501, italics added). As Friedman rightly observes, Conrad here provides "a remarkably rigid case of writing in parallels."[20]

Despite the asserted similarities between the dead man and the living one, there are still some crucial differences. Most obviously, although "disillusioned weariness" seeks the escape of death, "disenchanted vanity" requires revenge. Nostromo soon decides that the only appropriate recompense for the seemingly senseless betrayals he has been forced to commit is to claim for himself the whole treasure. It has been "paid for by a soul lost and by a vanished life" (p. 502). Furthermore, Nostromo insists, "there was no one in the world but Gian' Battista Fidanza, Capataz de Cargadores to pay such a price." "Nothing," he immediately asserts, "should be allowed now to rob him of his bargain" (p. 502).

The formerly incorruptible Nostromo thereby begins to become the ironically named faithless Captain Fidanza. The first indication of his transpiring metamorphosis is the asserted bargain. Nostromo did not contract to buy the treasure by leaving Teresa to die without a priest or by abandoning Decoud on the island, and certainly Gould did not consent to sell it on those same terms. Nostromo's bargain is really a rationalized reaction to his own sense of having been betrayed. Thus, on the island, he resembles Decoud in still another sense. Each refrains from directly confronting his own motives. The one who had "only the supreme illusion of a lover" (p. 189), had an illusion even more dominant, the illusion that he was a lover. The other, believing himself betrayed by the rich and thus entitled to his revenge, will not see the degree to which that first reaction is itself a betrayal of those whose main sin was simply to allow him to indulge his vanity. Nostromo himself chose to be most capably "their man." And neither will Captain Fidanza acknowledge the later even less defensible betrayals which derive from the first one.

But Nostromo's full name, Giovanni Battista Fidanza, which is more and more emphasized as *Nostromo* concludes, is doubly ironic and further connects him with Decoud. He is not just an unfaithful Fidanza. He is also a mock John the Baptist with no messianic message to preach. The religious symbolism suggested at this point in the novel is all parodic and reversed. This John the Baptist does not precede but follows a caricature Christ; he comes not to preach a new gospel but to subscribe himself to the already established one. "Those gentlemen talk about their gods," Decoud earlier observed, as a visiting Frenchman, among other men of affairs assembled in the Gould's great sala, "fell a prey to a screaming ecstasy that centered on 'ten million dollars' worth of copper practically in sight" (p. 199). Compared to this "preternatural" outburst, Nostromo's "I must grow rich very slowly" (p. 503) is the prevailing orthodoxy most modestly asserted.

Chapter ten in the third and final section of the book concludes with Nostromo enunciating his credo. The next chapter begins with an obviously contrasting observation. "Sulaco outstripped Nostromo's prudence, growing rich swiftly on the hidden treasures of the earth, hovered over by the anxious spirits of good and evil, torn out by the laboring hands of the people" (p. 504). As various critics have noted, Captain Fidanza embodies a basic pattern adhered to by others in his society and by that society itself. Friedman, for example, observes: "Indeed, everything that happens to Nostromo after the theft continues to become the pattern of experience for everyone else."[21] The previously quoted passages from the novel suggest, however, that even though Nostromo comes to worship at the established shrine, he does so as — to use the term Conrad stresses — a "prudent" communicant. And prudence doesn't save him any more than intelligence saved Decoud.

Although Nostromo is careful, Sulaco is not. The new country — experiencing "a second youth, like a new life, full of promise, of unrest, of toil, scattering lavishly its wealth to the four corners of the world" (p. 504) — can be personified, in some senses, more by the young Nostromo than by the mature Captain Fidanza. In the carelessness of his relative poverty, the Capataz de Cargadores also scattered what wealth he had, to be, as Teresa Viola saw, "an absurd spendthrift" (p. 254). She also foresaw the probable conclusion to the course of life he then followed. " 'They have turned your head with their praises,' gasped the sick woman. 'They have been paying you with words. Your folly shall betray you into poverty, misery, and starvation. The very leperos shall laugh at you — the great Capataz' " (p. 257). Partly prompted by her warning and increasingly aware of how the rich whom he serves have given him "a silly name — and nothing besides — in exchange for [his] soul and body" (p. 256), Nostromo does mend his extravagant ways. But he does so to die a death as ignoble as the one Teresa predicted, a death occasioned both by his careful and his country's more careless worship of wealth.

The thriving new Occidental Republic sees certain "material changes swept along in the train of material interests" (p. 504). One of these signs of progress is the lighthouse erected on the Great Isabel. This edifice, which provides the title for the concluding section of the novel, does not bring to light the manner whereby Captain Fidanza gradually enriches himself but it does illuminate the final consequences of that process. The lighthouse, constructed on the same island on which the silver is hidden, becomes an ironic comment on the change that has taken place in Nostromo's life. The man who previously insisted on living, as the illustrous Capataz of the Sulaco Cargadores, totally in the public eye now finds that even "the crew of his own schooner were to be feared as if they had been spies upon their dreaded captain" (p. 523). He discovers that he hates the stealth his situation forces upon him but he hates even more the idea of being (the symbolic import of the lighthouse) revealed. When he returned from a trading voyage to discover builders at work on the island, "he was struck with amazed dread at this turn of chance, that would kindle a far-reaching light upon the only secret spot of his life" (p. 525).

His first thought, and one which further connects him with Decoud, is to commit suicide. That temporizing act, however, would not be a final solution to the problem Nostromo faces. "He imagined himself dead, and the disgrace, the shame going on" (p. 525). So the ever resourceful Capataz soon contrives another plan. He asks that old Giorgio be appointed keeper of the light. Since he has done the Occidental Steam Navigation Company some service, his request is soon granted. Nostromo will even have, with this arrangement, obvious reason for often visiting the island. It is common knowledge that he and Linda shall eventually wed. But the stratagem designed to keep him from being "lost irretrievably" (p. 525), like other self-serving schemes embraced by other characters in *Nostromo,* fails completely.

Even before he confronts the problem of the lighthouse, Nostromo is painfully aware of how false his life has become. "A crime," the narrator tells us, "entering a man's existence, eats it up like a malignant growth, consumes it like a fever" (p. 523). And more specifically, "Nostromo had lost his peace; the genuineness of all his qualities was destroyed.... His courage, his magnificence, his leisure, his work, everything was as before." Except for one crucial difference: "everything was a sham" (pp. 523-24). Only "the treasure was real" (p. 524). As he nears his unanticipated end, Nostromo insists on that one "reality," just as Decoud, finally (but in a different sense), believed only in silver. At the same time Captain Fidanza also hates what the treasure is doing to him. He cannot sustain the burden of duplicity inherent in his life and hopes that somehow it can be made lighter by being shared. In short, he requires a wife who "would have to know his secret or else life would be impossible" (p. 524).

Nostromo has also decided that Linda cannot be that wife. To start with, she is her father's daughter, "all fire and words, touched with gloom and scorn, a chip of the old block, true daughter of the austere republican" (p. 524). Completely committed to meeting the demands of duty, she can hardly be a partner in dishonesty and duplicity. Indeed, the novel ends with her still, despite the recent tragedy of Nostromo's death, tending the light that "burned unfailing above the lost treasure of the San Tomé mine" (p. 565). Nostromo knows that her love, were she his wife, would be above all, "uncompromising — like her soul" (p. 524). He is too much compromised to cope with such devotion. Furthermore, Linda is also very much her mother's daughter. Nostromo and Giorgio both note the degree to which she looks and sounds like the dead Teresa. To her father, "her deep, vibrating 'Eh, Padre?' seemed, but for the change of the word, the very echo of the impassioned, remonstrating 'Eh, Giorgio?' of poor Signora Teresa" (p. 529). When required, so he believes, to propose to the elder daughter and not the preferred, more complacent Giselle, Nostromo also notes that Linda "pronounced [his] name exactly with her mother's intonation" (p. 532).

This detail is an effective example of how carefully Conrad structures *Nostromo*. The daughter's pronounciation of the name recalls the mother's, and the mother last spoke to Nostromo some three hundred pages earlier in the novel. What she said when she then addressed him by name has already been briefly noted but can here be quoted in full: "Get riches at least for once, you indispensable, admired Gian' Battista, to whom the peace of a dying woman is less than the praise of people who have given you a silly name — and nothing besides — in exchange for your soul and body" (p. 256). Signora Teresa accurately predicted the bankruptcy in which Nostromo's first course of action must conclude. But "getting riches" only led to a different far more devastating bankruptcy. Small wonder Nostromo cannot love the girl whose voice itself is a continuation of her mother's earlier condemnation but whose standards would deplore the manner in which he has heeded the mother's counsel. When he hears Linda accept his forced proposal and say his name, unsurprisingly, "a gloom as of the grave covered Nostromo's heart" (p. 532).

The lighthouse forces Nostromo to arrange for the Violas to live on the Great Isabel to tend the light. Their presence there means that he must have some public reason for regularly visiting the island. So the solution designed to keep the disgrace of his life hidden requires Captain Fidanza to act even more dishonestly than he did while simply growing rich on the stolen silver. Then he could at least pretend that he had a claim on the treasure. But more and more he finds that it claims him, a fate earlier foreshadowed when the narrator described Nostromo's first return to the island and the silver buried there: "And the spirits of good and evil that hover about a forbidden treasure understood well that the silver of the San Tomé was provided now with a faithful and lifelong slave" (p. 501).

In the service of the silver, Nostromo reveals a craven timorousness utterly uncharacteristic of the earlier indomitable Capataz de Cargadores. The man who would face the most arduous tasks — the sailor who could save for others the shipload of silver, the messenger who could ride overland "four hundred miles in six days, through a disturbed country, ending by the feat of passing through the Monterist lines outside Cayta" (p. 482) to summon Barios and thus save (again for others) the whole mountain of silver and Sulaco itself — this former hero cannot at last even "utter the name in his mind" of the girl he wanted to marry. "He was afraid of being forbidden the island" (p. 531). Because "the shining spectre of the treasure" claims "his allegiance in a silence that could not be gainsaid" (p. 531), Nostromo allows Giorgio to assume that the proposal he came to make was intended all along for Linda. Decoud, in his engagement to Antonia, was unconsciously self-deceived. Nostromo, in his engagement to Linda, is consciously deceiving. As Juliet McLaughlan rightly observes: "The 'incorruptible' Nostromo has become corrupt, and the full ugliness of his corruption appears in the needless suffering of Linda Viola: this is the measure of his total degradation."[22]

Betrothed to the elder daughter, Nostromo nevertheless and at once commences his formal wooing of her younger sister. Linda has hardly left the room to return to her duty of tending the light before Nostromo is showering Giselle with such banal compliments as "your hair like gold, and your eyes like violets, and your lips like the rose" (p. 535). But even though he confesses his love for the younger sister, he will not accede to her plea that he carry her away from Linda and the island that very night. A treasure, he tells her, "stands between us two and the freedom of the world" (p. 539). By partly confessing how he acquired that treasure, he thinks he has freed himself from it. When Giselle, however, asks where the silver is hidden, he cannot tell her.

He thereby realizes that "he had not regained his freedom," and "his soul died within him at the vision of himself creeping in presently along the ravine." Come night, he shall, he foresees, be doing the "work of a craven slave." He will be "creeping in, determined in a purpose that numbed his breast, and creeping out again loaded with silver" (p. 542). Like Decoud, this self-proclaimed lover is false. Also like Decoud, he will tear treasure (the same treasure even) from the earth to find that this treasure brings not a richer life but death. It might also be noted that just as Nostromo here doubly resembles Decoud, so too does Charles Gould resemble Nostromo. Most obviously, "Gould's libidinous energies are [increasingly] engaged in the mine."[23] As with Nostromo, the engagement saps him of his humanity even as it raises him in his world — in Gould's case to the high position of *el rey de Sulaco*. Edward Said sums up this inverse relationship: "The more [Gould] is a king, the less able he is to know what a slave he really is."[24] In effect, then, Gould's justification for mining the silver is reified and undermined by Nostromo's remining of much that same silver. As Eloise Hay notes, "Nostromo, and this explains his name in the title, emerges as the great manifestation and test of Gould's proposition — that the silver can be made an agent of moral reform."[25]

Silver was also to be a force for freedom, but here too the novel's title is significant, for it points the way to how all the characters reflect one another as flawed, counterfeit. Peter Christmas observes that " 'our man' implies an owner, one who has the freedom which authority over others implies. But who is whose man in Nostromo? Gould is 'our man' to Holroyd, Ribiera is 'our man' to Gould, and so on down the line. Captain Mitchell may 'lend' Nostromo out to oblige his friends, but who runs the dockyard, Gian' Battista or 'Fussy Joe'?" As Christmas continues, "everyone pretends that another man is 'our man' on the false assumption that all inhabit a realm of freedom.

Even the crown of this hierarchy of apparent control, the sickly Holroyd, working himself to death in an office thousands of miles away, has for his sole conscious aim merely the introduction to Latin America of the Christianity of a Rotary Club."[26] What most keeps this game going is the flow of silver and the promise of freedom implicit in the prospect of wealth. Yet Nostromo, it will be recalled, could be free with his silver only when all that he had of it were the few buttons that he bestowed on the brazen Paquita who, practically a woman of the streets and not particularly dear to him, publicly claimed a gift. "You shall have your present; and so that everyone should know who is your lover to-day, you may cut all the silver buttons off my coat" (p. 129), he tells her, and she proceeds to do so. When he has far more wealth than he needs and finds his hidden hoard of silver an intolerable burden, he still cannot give it up for the woman he thinks he really loves. The one-time master of silver has become its slave.

"In the last two chapters," Friedman observes, "the novel comes to rest squarely on the character of Nostromo. Until now the events in which he has figured to have been webbed in suggestive patterns. His experience is now discovered to be at the exact center of the web, and the book closes — as it has all along suggested it would — with Nostromo."[27] This observation is substantially accurate and helps refute Guerard's claim that the novel's "greatest defect is that it is at least two hundred pages too long" as well as G.W. Spence's countering contention "that *Nostromo* is about one hundred pages too short." The first of these critics argues that "the large themes" in the book "have been fully developed" in the first two parts of the novel and thus overlooks the subtle patterns worked out in the final section, while the second wants all that which is subtly suggested in the third part of *Nostromo* to be explicitly stated so that there might be "a sufficient rendering of the theme in economic and political action."[28] But the third part of the novel is integral to the work as a whole; what is set forth there is "sufficiently rendered."

Nevertheless, Friedman's argument that Nostromo finally comes to embody all the essential patterns established in the novel should be qualified. In some ways Decoud continues to be the character most obviously situated at the heart of the web, and this is especially true with respect to Nostromo's demise. Like Decoud, Nostromo finally dies a double death — drowned in one sense and shot in another. The Capataz's death can even be viewed as the inverse of the boulevardier's. Decoud drowns because of a self-inflicted shot. Nostromo is shot because of a self-inflicted figurative drowning. Conrad also makes the Capataz's metaphoric drowning incontrovertibly obvious. After declaring his love for Giselle, Nostromo, later that same night, "creeping out of the ravine, weighted with silver," sees a light in the younger sister's window and comes to her but not, as she hopes, "to carry [her] off." He must be prudent and first "grow rich slowly." That prudence, however, is not consistent with the way he embraces the girl. "The magnificent Capataz clasped her round her white neck in the darkness of the gulf as a drowning man clutches at a straw" (pp. 544-45).

Nostromo cannot be saved by the pliant Giselle; no more than Decoud could be kept alive by Antonia who was rather more substantial than Giselle; no more than Charles Gould, at the end of the novel, can be rescued by his almost ideal wife from the consequences of his infatuation with his mine. Giselle, declaring her love, only emphasizes the predicament in which her beloved finds himself. "Your love is to me like your treasure is to you. It is there, but I can never get enough of it" (p. 547). The love and the treasure are similar in several other ways too. Most obviously, both are secret. They are also secret for the same reason. Because Nostromo is, as Leo Gurko notes, "a thief of both money and love," the love, like the treasure, must remain hidden.[29] Giselle's comparison applies in still another way too. The dream of love, like the dream of treasure, promises total and perpetual fulfillment, but neither dream, in *Nostromo*, provides any enduring happiness.[30]

Indeed, just as characters deceive themselves as to the nature of their actions and situation by idealizing or spiritualizing the material (Charles Gould is the most obvious example), so too can they mislead themselves by attempting to materialize the spiritual (Nostromo, for example, weighs his love for Giselle in the same balance with the treasure and finds love wanting). The chief engineer, trained to see things as they are, was therefore only partly correct when he earlier observed that "things seem to be worth nothing by what they are in themselves" in that, as he went on to maintain, "the only solid thing about" anything is its "spiritual value" (p. 318). Material values can be very solid indeed. In fact, whether the universe is assessed in terms of supposed spiritual or material values, material considerations generally carry the day. And the ultimate consequence of material considerations — as Decoud earlier recognized, as Dr. Monygham finally attests, as the death of Nostromo demonstrates — is destruction and death.

Still figuratively drowning, intent on removing more silver from the island, Nostromo, near "the tree under which Martin Decoud spent his last days, beholding life like a succession of senseless images" (p. 553), is mistakenly shot by Giorgio Viola. The setting of the "accident" is appropriate and not just because it further connects the deaths of Decoud and Nostromo. The former's final vision is partly vindicated by the latter's death, which is, in most respects, absurd. The old Garibaldino, ostensibly committed to a belief in the common man, will allow no "man of the people" to court his younger daughter. But neither will he tell Nostromo about the danger that he thinks Ramirez represents. "A touch of senile vanity" prompts him to prove "that he was equal yet to the task of guarding alone the honor of his house" (p. 548). Giselle, aware of her father's recent armed night-time watchings and wanderings, requires Nostromo to promise that he will not visit her that evening. But he, faithless to the end, breaks that promise and then, shot, lies magnificently when he explains why he did so. "It seemed as though I could not live through the night without seeing thee once more — my star, my little flower" (p. 554). And Giorgio's almost simultaneous explanation of what he is certain he has done is equally inaccurate, although unconsciously so. "I have shot Ramirez — *infame!*" he tells Linda, as she too arrives on the scene. "Like a thief he came, and like a thief he fell. The child had to be protected" (p. 554).

The old man is not, of course, completely wrong. "Mistaken for an undesirable suitor of Giselle's (which in fact he is), [Nostromo] is shot down like a thief (which indeed he is also) by her father and his patron."[31] There is a certain paradoxical logic to Nostromo's death even though it derives from a series of more or less senseless mistakes and misjudgments. The first and most basic of these errors is Nostromo's misestimation of the value of silver, a misvaluation that leads him to his death and continues beyond it. When he offers what is, in effect, a deathbed confession to the "monastically hooded" (p. 558) Mrs. Gould whom he has summoned to hear that confession, he thinks he can free himself by admitting his robbery and claims that he could have renounced the treasure for Giselle. But escape is not that easy, and Nostromo soon takes a different tone towards his unlawful treasure. "Alas! it holds me yet" (p. 559). He cannot, even while dying, renounce the silver that made him a thief, that caused him to die like a thief. " 'I die betrayed — betrayed by —' But he did not say by whom or what he was dying betrayed" (p. 559). Which is hardly surprising; on the simplest level, he betrayed himself.

In betraying himself, he has necessarily betrayed others. "The child had to be protected," the father insisted. These words should recall the same mission previously laid on Nostromo. Earlier in the novel, Nostromo briefly visited old Viola before departing on his crucial journey to summon Barios. While being served a "beggar's fare" of "a few dry crusts of bread and half a raw onion" (p. 470), while thinking of his present poverty and painfully contemplating the fact that a treasure then lay buried on the Great Isabel, Nostromo listened to the old man tell of his wife's death. Her last action was, when she heard the sound of a shot, to call upon Nostromo "to save the children" (p. 470). Contrary to what he later claims, Nostromo did not betray the dying woman only when, with some reason, he refused to bring her a priest. He really betrays Teresa when he chooses the silver over Giselle, when he chooses Giselle over Linda but lacks the courage to say so.[32] In other words, Nostromo, as earlier noted, pretends that a forced betrayal entitles him to keep the silver, but the betrayal that ostensibly justified his crime comes more after the deed than before it. Because of the silver, he betrays all the Violas and especially Teresa. Far from saving the children as she asked, he acts in such a fashion that he puts one of them once — admittedly a rather meodramatic action — literally at the other's throat and leaves them both the fullest measure of sorrow that they can bear.

Old Viola never realizes that he killed Nostromo but he does note that somehow the dying man "cried out in son Gian' Battista's voice" (p. 563). These words also suggest another basic pattern that is fully established at the conclusion of *Nostromo*. Nostromo, it will be remembered, was not just the Violas' prospective son-in-law. He was also, especially for Giorgio Viola, a substitute son to take the place of the real son who died as a child but who would have been had he lived, Giorgio regularly insists, the same man that Nostromo is. Fathers and sons, however, do not fare very well in the world of *Nostromo*. The Goulds, father and son, are, early in the novel, divided because of the San Tomé silver mine. As the son sees, the concession forced onto his father destroys the father's life. Nevertheless, the son disregards the dying man's injunction and returns to Costaguana, partly to avenge his father and partly to prove that he can cope with the mine. But because of his determination to make something of the mine, the son is, as Edward Said points out, "victimized by an endless vicious circle of activity as completely as his father was by the futility of South America."[33] Mrs. Gould puts the same matter another way: "The energetic spirit of the son" is mastered by the San Tomé mine just "as it had mastered the lamentable weakness of the father" (p. 522). Charles Gould is, in one sense, victimized even more than was his father. He becomes so obsessed with the mine that, not surprisingly (he is regularly seen leaving his wife to spend the night at the mountain), he will have no son. So in each case, Nostromo's and Charles Gould's, an obsession with silver leads to the destruction of an existing father and son relationship and a breech with ongoing life. Neither son shall become a father; each man ends up married much more to the metal than to the woman he claims to love.

The question originally asked — what, really, is the effect of the silver? — can at last be conclusively answered. The Occidental Republic may, for a time, enjoy prosperity. The new state may seem politically stable. But even then, on a more basic level, the silver perverts the real relationships of life, those on which the continuation of human existence depends.[34] Material interests sever generations and divide husband and wife — woman and man. Indeed, Nostromo's death puts an end to both his promised marriage and his impending affair. Linda, like Antonia, is widowed without ever having been a bride, while Mrs. Gould, as another abandoned woman, can "console" the grief-stricken Giselle: "Very soon he would have forgotten you for his treasure." She speaks with authority. When the young girl argues that Nostromo loved her "as no one had ever been loved before," the older woman answers only, "I have been loved too" (p. 561). She knows the "immense desolation" of living "all alone in the Treasure House of the World" (p. 522).

The novel appropriately ends with Linda's cry of incomprehension and grief. "I cannot understand. I cannot understand. But I shall never forget thee. Never! . . . Never! Gian' Battista!" (p. 566). Only Dr. Monygham, who has just "been defeated [when Mrs. Gould claims that Nostromo told her nothing] by the magnificent Capataz de Cargadores" (p. 561) and defeated in the presence of the woman he secretly loves, can see in Linda's lamentation another victory for Nostromo. "In that true cry of undying passion. . . . The genius of the magnificent Capataz de Cargadores dominated the dark gulf containing his conquests of treasure and love" (p. 566). The cry may be true but the gulf is still dark and neither the treasure nor the love was conquered. Both were stolen; neither was mastered. As Said maintains: "No better ending for the novel could have been written." Across "a silent world of immense, empty spaces" comes "an incoherent cry, which symbolizes mankind's inarticulate sadness over itself."[35] Linda expresses the hopeless disparity between her dream of love and the disaster of Nostromo's death. Other dreams, especially the dream of treasure, are, *Nostromo* demonstrates, equally hopeless, equally tragic.[36]

Such is the conclusion of *Nostromo.* But even though various patterns become clear, the book does not really end. Dreams and revolutions will continue. In fact, the groundwork for yet another revolution is being laid in the last chapters of the novel, and this one is designed, appropriately, to undo precisely what the previous revolution accomplished. What is even more ironic is that Martin Decoud, who thought politics a farce, becomes, when dead, one of the founding fathers of the Occidental Republic, and it is in his name that the next uprising is being promoted. With "invincible resolution," Antonia insists "that this [to 'annex the rest of Costaguana to the order and prosperity of Sulaco'] was from the first poor Martin's intention" (p. 509). Poor Martin, we have seen, never really intended anything except to effect his own suicide. The farce of politics, his spirit might observe, still rolls tragically on.

Certainly, the most common figure encountered in *Nostromo* is a circle. On the individual level, various characters trace abortive voyages to end very much where they began. On the public level, "history is proved to be cyclical" and "not in accord with Gould's dreams of a progressive capitalism."[37] Nothing, as Howe insists, is final: "the civil war brings capitalism and capitalism will bring civil war, progress *has* come out of chaos but it is the kind of progress likely to end in chaos."[38] And neither is there, despite Captain Mitchell's claims to the contrary, any great lineal development in *Nostromo.* As Royal Roussel argues, "the narrator, who frames the story of Gould against the darkness which is at once its source and end, sees that Mitchell's sense of historical progress is an illusion. The real movement of history for him is not linear but cyclical." Moreover, Mitchell's oft repeated tale of progress itself "takes on a certain circularity."[39] Story follows story just as revolution follows revolution.[40] A *revolution*, in fact, provides a perfect focus for the novel. The one event around which much of the action in the book centers is summary, symbol, and objective correlative for the whole novel and for most of the separate episodes.

The novel itself exhibits this same circular form. One of Conrad's most subtle touches comes at the very end when he describes how Linda's cry "seemed to ring aloud from Punta Mala to Azuera and away to the bright line of the horizon, overhung by a big white cloud shining like a mass of solid silver" (p. 566). Azuera, of course, suggests the "two gringos, spectral and alive," who cannot leave "its forbidden wealth" (p. 5). At the end of the novel they have been replaced by Nostromo and Charles Gould. These two also embody paradoxes — Nostromo achieves victory in defeat, Gould finds defeat in victory — and both are slaves to silver. But it is the "white cloud shining like a mass of solid silver" that most connects the end of *Nostromo* to the beginnning. The epigraph of the novel, given on the title page, reads: "So foul a sky clears not without a storm." Yet, as Winifred Lynskey observes, "the storm of revolution in *Nostromo* has not cleared a sky darkened by material interests.... The storm is yet to come."[41] More accurately, at the conclusion of the book the sky is clouding again to be what it was at the beginning. As effectively as Joyce in *Finnegans Wake*, Conrad works *Nostromo* into a circle and sets that circle spinning.[42]

But what, finally, is most striking about that last spinning is the prophetic note of its ominous whir. A recent study of the novel as a study of history concludes that "the dubious character of the dying Nostromo's legacy to Linda" constitutes "a foreboding that an intellectual trajectory has been set in motion whose shape we might sketch, with the benefit of our hindsight, by the mere chronological listing of a few representative names: Lamartine, Proudhon, Garibaldi, Kropotkin, Plekhanov, Trotsky, Lenin, Stalin." For this critic: "The qualitative change implicit in this list is the greatest fear which Conrad put into *Nostromo*. For the whole work is devoted to demonstrating that . . . economic law is just as doomed as revolutionary violence so far as the creation of a civilized society is concerned, and for the same reason. If one celebrates the necessity of a perpetual strife of class interest while the other relies on a myth of contractual sanctity to underwrite its systematized egotism, both are materialistic and function only by exploiting the baser instincts of mankind."[43] As earlier observed, nothing in the novel refutes Dr. Monygham's prognosis for the Occidental Republic, and nothing in the twentieth century refutes Conrad's prognosis either — Battista, Papa Doc, Somoza, Pinochet, the CIA, the Dirty War, the death squads.

3

Levels of Plotting in *The Secret Agent*

The Secret Agent, Jackson Heimer has argued, is a kind of shrunken *Nostromo.* Both books, for this critic, center on betrayal, but that subject is "painted [in the later work] on a much smaller canvas." The "background" of *Nostromo,* "mysterious and vast, beautiful and overpowering," carries over to the novel itself, whereas "*The Secret Agent,* by contrast, takes place in an atmosphere that is confined, sordid and ugly." The seriousness of the issues in this text are reduced to the "petty and grubby" by the very setting in which they are examined and then the author's " 'ironic method' . . . reduces them still further."[1] The result, Heimer claims, is "one of the gloomiest of Conrad's novels" and one of the less consequential: compared to the high seriousness of *Nostromo* ("grandiose and lofty, grand and idealistic") what happens in *The Secret Agent* "hardly seems to matter to anyone."[2] Other critics would concur with Heimer's estimation of the darkness of the vision in the latter novel — "this fiercely controlled work of an unusually carbolic nature"; "the most grim of Conrad's novels"; "Conrad's bleakest book"[3] — but not all would agree with his estimation of the scope and significance of that dark vision. F.R. Leavis deemed *The Secret Agent* "indubitably a classic and a masterpiece," and Leavis's judgment in these matters cannot be lightly dismissed.[4] J. Hillis Miller finds the same novel to be "one of [Conrad's] most impressive dramatizations of [his] black view of civilized society."[5] Still more recently, H.M. Daleski judges this book to be Conrad's "finest artistic achievement."[6] And Conrad himself, it might be added, thought the novel one of his best.[7]

But the comparison with *Nostromo* is still germane. Both novels, for example, have an obvious political focus, and in each Conrad's assessment of the absurdity of political action centers on revolution and revolutionaries. Furthermore, although betrayal, as Heimer rightly notes, plays an important role in the two novels, that act does not really characterize the moral universe of either work. Betrayal, in Heimer's large sense, demands a pervasive prior code. There must, after all, be accepted standards of how the individual should act before those standards can be betrayed. But in neither *Nostromo* nor *The Secret Agent* can we catch the author privileging any particular code by the way he portrays his characters transgressing against it. On the contrary, it is the transgressions that are privileged, that demonstrate the nullities of the accepted codes. As Chief Inspector Heat maintains, most crimes affirm the established "constitution of society."[8] Confronting his clientele, Heat can recognize "his fellow-citizens gone wrong" (p. 92), but not so wrong that they do not submit in their own profession to the same "morality" that he maintains in his. This officer of the law is backed up by the narrator of the novel who also notes that "the mind and the instincts of a burglar are of the same kind as the mind and the instincts of a police officer," that they are both "products of the same machine" and "both recognize the same conventions" (p. 92). "Conventions" are, then, exactly what the term implies, merely conventional. In other words, as Joseph Wiesenfarth points out, "*The Secret Agent* is totally devoid of a significant and accepted moral order."[9] *Nostromo* too evinces the same lack.

Even the differences in the setting of the two novels are not that great. In his preface to *The Secret Agent* Conrad speaks of "musing" before various "phenomenon." He mentions "South America, a continent of crude sunshine and brutal revolutions." Equally suggestive is "the sea, the vast expanse of salt waters, the mirror of heaven's frowns and smiles." But he soon passes to quite a different topic. "Then the vision of an enormous town presented itself, of a monstrous town more populous than some continents and in its man-made might as if indifferent to heaven's frowns and smiles; a cruel devourer of the world's light." This town, the setting for *The Secret Agent,* well may be "sordid and ugly" but it is hardly confined. Indeed, Conrad continues: "There was room enough there to place any story, depth enough there for any passion, variety enough there for any setting, darkness enough to bury five millions of lives" (p. xii).

So we have a crucial difference after all. Treasure was excavated in one setting. Lives are buried in the other. *Nostromo* is, in this sense, Conrad's fullest study of man as maker, of man as (acting on the largest level and attempting to determine the destiny of continents) imperialist. *The Secret Agent* portrays the fate of those who must live with what materialistic-minded men have done. "The impersonal, dehumanized city," the world of modern man, contains, Conrad suggests in *The Secret Agent,* myriads of "individual men and women struggling vainly to assert their identity, to make themselves felt, their presence known, amid the overwhelming anonymity of city life, which ... was the essence of human existence in London."[10] Representative of all those anonymous humans are the Verlocs. As in *Nostromo,* a little world reflects a larger one, but the primary focus is reversed and is now on the most microcosmic of characters. It is as if Conrad is attempting a novel on the same scope and scale as *Nostromo* but a novel such as *Nostromo* might be were the narrative centers provided by, say, Rameriz and the "blood-thirsty" little hater of capitalists."

The Verlocs are representative but representative of what? Their marriage, "founded as it is on a systematic reciprocity of incomprehension, achieves an unusual degree of representative significance" to be, for this same critic, "a microcosmic representation of a society in which every man is a kind of fifth columnist to his neighbor."[11] Jacques Berthoud thus stresses what numerous other commentators have noted, that every character in the novel is largely in the dark about every other character. From this point of view, the novel is almost a textbook study of misinformation theory.[12] Miller, however, would locate the heart of the text's representativeness somewhere else: "Mr. Verloc, secret agent, at once respectable bourgeois shopkeeper and family man, member of various revolutionary societies, *agent provocateur* for a reactionary foreign power, and unofficial spy for the British police, is a perfect example of the sinister connectedness of all levels of society from bottom to top, from the far left to the far right." Through Verloc, "Conrad sees [and shows] all society as rotten at the core."[13] Or instead of the husband at the heart of the novel, we can have the wife: "Winnie's story . . . may be thought of as the paradigmatic center of a series of concentric circles. The larger vacancy with which the novelist is concerned is a social vacancy, a social loss of self, as it were, that expresses itself in the nullity of a pervasive and darkly corrupting moral nihilism and is itself a form of social madness or breakdown."[14] Or we might posit Stevie, or Sir Ethelred, or the Professor, or even perhaps Ossipon as the core of the novel. With empty circles spinning everywhere, it is hard to pick one as central to all the rest.[15]

But the "corruscating whirl of circles" (p. 49) does begin to fall more clearly into some pattern as the novel winds to its conclusion. By the beginning of chapter eleven, Stevie has been blown up; Verloc's plot has been discovered; Mrs. Verloc has learned, thanks to Inspector Heat, of the fate of her brother. All that remains is for the Verlocs to confront one another and work out a way in which they might survive their catastrophe. Before such a confrontation takes place, however, Conrad examines the mental state of Mr. Verloc. He "was shaken morally to pieces" that his brother-in-law had been blown literally to pieces (p. 230). He had foreseen everything except the possibility that Stevie might stumble and "death, whose catastrophic character cannot be argued away by sophisticated reasoning or pervasive eloquence" (p. 229).[16] Soon Verloc also recalls something else he had earlier overlooked. He had not particularly noted his wife's statement that he was not to worry if Stevie got lost. Now he knows what she meant. His wife had sewn their address into her brother's coat. So Stevie, completely lost, still "turned up with a vengeance" (p. 230). When Verloc tries to console Winnie for the death of her brother, he is, therefore, himself in a complex emotional state. He partly desires to comfort her and assure her that he did not intend any harm to come to Stevie, while, at the same time, he also partly blames her for the difficulty that he is in. He will surely be arrested; the best he can hope for is a two-year sentence. If he can forgive her, she should forgive him.

The scene that ensues is part of a larger pattern. As John Hagan points out, this interview between husband and wife corresponds to other imperfect interviews in that always "the two persons involved are working radically at cross-purposes."[17] Characters never effectively communicate, never understand one another or sympathize with another's feelings. The final encounter between husband and wife is, therefore, no different from earlier ones, even though, as Hagan also notes, it reverses their first scenes together. Previously Winnie talked of Stevie, while Verloc could not or would not explain his personal difficulties. Now Verloc talks of his own predicament and of Stevie, while Winnie will not, cannot, explain her grief. A tragedy has befallen the marriage and it is still, strangely, very much the same marriage that it earlier was. Even less likely, the Verlocs' marriage is explicitly designated as the pattern for other marriages but only in what we might term its postlapsarian state. With a touch of grimness, the Assistant Commissioner investigating the bomb outrage observed to Sir Ethelred that the prime suspect was not likely to flee, for they were really dealing with "a domestic drama" (p. 222). His grimness derived from his recognition that, like Verloc, he too could not leave London because of a "genuine wife," and "nothing could be more characteristic of the respectable bond than that" (p. 221).

With the exception of the Professor, all of the anarchists are lazily content to allow others, especially women, to support them. Verloc, however, is honorably married. Although tending to sloth, he still maintains both his wife and her family. To do so, he keeps a shop, a respectable bourgeois occupation (even though most of the wares he sells are shady). He also serves as a secret agent but one firmly on the side of propriety, unofficially a spy for the British police and officially an agent who keeps track of anarchists for a reactionary Continental government. What he betrays is, after all, "the secret and *unlawful* proceedings of his fellow-men" (p. 245, emphasis added). He is, as Paul Kirschner notes, "neither a revolutionary nor a reformer. In his modest way he is a conservative."[18]

There is, therefore, nothing particularly unusual about Verloc's being married, even though he pretends to be an anarchist. Nor is his marriage in any sense distinctive. The Verlocs at first, as David Daiches observes, live in "a little domestic society" that, "with its familiar routine, its satisfactory mutual adjustments, its devices for pandering to the secret needs of each one of its members, seems to work and actually does work until it is forced apart in the most violent way by the sudden revelation of those secret needs."[19] In this little society, Verloc is, as a husband, no doubt typical. Although he had "grown older, fatter, heavier," he still believed that he "lacked no fascination for being loved for his own sake" (p. 252). Any man might suffer from a similar delusion. Thus, when a revelation comes, it comes to someone who never dreamed such a revelation was possible. Verloc dies with his "note of wooing" on his lips. And this fact represents, for Daiches, the most disturbing aspect of the book. The murder, set in such a context of "marital intimacy," suggests "that all such intimacy is both illusory and squalid."[20]

Verloc was a respectably married man. Yet his "steady fidelity to his own fireside" still had "a character of unceremonious impermanency" achieved through his ever present hat (p. 175). The roles of husband and wife, however, are soon reversed in this respect too. In their final scene, the wife, "with her hat and veil," has "the air of a visitor, of having looked in on Mr. Verloc for a moment" (p. 255). But Conrad again demonstrates that nothing is really changed. The lives of all characters are so isolated that even partners in marriage are still transient strangers. Claire Rosenfield rightly insists that "in a world where the brother plays the son and complete isolation substitutes for sexual fulfillment between husband and wife, love itself is demonic and destructive."[21] Domesticity is finally not love, nor even sex, but the carving knife used to kill. The larger world of politics, of Embassy plots, of obtuse Home Secretaries, of interchangeable police and thieves is an insane world. And the smaller world of domesticity is equally insane. At the end of the novel, the little society, as much as the great one, is shown to be "terrible and crazy and incomprehensible."[22]

The incomprehensible nature of both worlds is especially suggested by the inability of any character to master either. For all, nothing turns out as intended. The Professor builds his bombs to advance the cause of anarchy and any anarchist is welcome to use them. But the only bomb that explodes in the novel is employed in a scheme to force England to be more reactionary and to curtail the freedom of anarchists. Yet, when that bomb goes off, only Stevie is blown up. Vladimir's plot doubly fails. Greenwich Observatory survives. The public is not at all outraged by a bomb directed at science, the "fetish" of the day. Yet even though the machinations of Vladimir are uncovered, the Assistant Commissioner still cannot carry out his project to clear "this country of all the foreign political spies, police, and that sort of — of — dogs" (p. 226). The "prosecution of Verloc" was going to "demonstrate to the public both the danger and the indecency" of what had actually transpired (p. 226). Verloc's murder forestalls any such trial.

A character's inability to understand his world, to cope with an existence that is both terrible and crazy, is as evident in private life as in public. For example, in his first interview with Vladimir, Verloc admits to a previous unfortunate infatuation. He was betrayed then, but he is now, he maintains, too old to be similarly misled. He is, of course, mistaken. The first woman, after taking his money, sold him to the police. His wife takes his money and then kills him. Verloc, in the same interview with Vladimir, also maintains that he is trusted because of his voice. Yet when he, "for the first time in his life," attempts to take his wife "into his confidence" (p. 239), his voice is only "veiled sound" that "lapped against Mrs. Verloc's head as if it had been a head of stone" (p. 260). She will not even hear him, much less trust him.

This same pattern of misunderstanding is shown when Verloc cannot "possibly comprehend the value of Stevie in the eyes of Mrs. Verloc," since he mistakenly believes "that the value of individuals consists in what they are in themselves" (p. 233). He, naturally, never asks what he is in himself and how he should be accordingly valued. Other comments are equally indicative of how little he understands his own immediate situation. He notices the "wifely forethought" that left out both the plate of cold beef and the carving knife too (p. 231). He, talking of his dangerous profession, tells Winnie how he would not "worry a woman that's fond of me" over "the risk of having a knife stuck into me any time these seven years we've been married" (p. 197). He will teach his betrayers a lesson when he testifies at his trial. "Nothing on earth can stop me now," he claims, "looking fixedly at his wife, who was looking fixedly at a blank wall" (p. 245). Caught up with the problem of Vladimir's directive and the probable prison term which will come from Stevie's slip, Verloc does not perceive that the smaller setbacks prompting his comments are really leading to a much larger tragedy. He is attempting to console his wife even as she readies to kill him.

Verloc's illusion, the idea that he is loved for himself, has been seen as the cause of his death.[23] More obviously, however, his wife kills him, and she kills him not for his illusions but for hers, which are rather more complicated than the mere illusory belief that her husband has murdered her brother. As Verloc tries, ineptly, to comfort her — "You go to bed now. What you want is a good cry" (p. 241) — certain thoughts pass through Winnie's mind. Prompted by her "maternal and violent" temperament, she thinks first of her past childhood life as Stevie's protector. "It was a crushing memory" of "countless breakfast trays," "innumerable stairs," "endless drudgery" (p. 242), but drudgery partly redeemed by one dream of romance. This breath of relief, such as it was, represented Winnie's first consoling illusion. She might have married a young butcher to be his "girl-partner at the oar" in a fascinating "voyage down the sparkling stream of life" (p. 243). Perhaps she rather exaggerated the joys of sharing a butcher's life, but then the matter was never put to the test. Winnie cannot marry the young butcher. He could not support Stevie. Therefore, in marrying Verloc, she merely substitutes one imperfect situation for another.[24]

Conrad then shows how Winnie's different situation entails different illusions. She is, as Verloc's wife, well aware of "the occasional passage of Comrade Ossipon, the robust anarchist with shamelessly inviting eyes" (p. 243). His looks obviously invite her to experience with him whatever her husband does not provide, to substitute a young, robust male for a fat and slothful one. The degree to which she throws herself at Ossipon when she encounters him after the murder and her willingness to live with him on any terms suggest how appealing that invitation is. Because of Stevie, however, she cannot elope with Ossipon in the present any more than she could marry her butcher in the past. So she remains with Verloc, justifying such fidelity with "the supreme illusion of her life"; Verloc and Stevie "might have been father and son" (p. 244).

The illusion, Conrad demonstrates, is supreme in two distinct senses. It is, first, a most exaggerated view of the facts. Verloc is fat and dark with a heavy black mustache; Stevie is slim and fair and has a wispy blond beard; the two could hardly look less like father and son. But the illusion is also supreme in a second sense. It is most necessary because it provides some rationale for Winnie's frustrating life and seems to justify her existence as a woman. If Verloc can be seen as the boy's father, then she, Verloc's wife, who really resembles Stevie, might well be his mother. Her marriage would then be real. The proof for its validity, however, would not have to depend on any relationship between husband and wife but could be embodied in the "son." Stevie, cast in this role, would attest to the sexual capability of the mother.[25]

This supreme illusion, although complex, still resembles the two simpler ones. All attest to how unimportant Verloc is in his wife's life and how only illusion justifies his presence there. His existence, moreover, completely conflicts with the illusion that compensates for him (he is the husband, so Ossipon, like the young butcher, must be a might-have-been) and largely conflicts with the illusion that justifies him (he does not really resemble Stevie at all). When the death of Stevie terminates the necessity for such illusion, it is not surprising that the wife turns immediately against her husband and does so largely on the level of illusion too. Winnie dramatically insists that Verloc deliberately killed Stevie. "This man took the boy away to murder him. He took the boy away from his home to murder him. He took the boy away from me to murder him" (p. 246).

Mrs. Verloc does not act on this gross misreading of Mr. Verloc's motives until the end of their encounter. At first, on a quite rational level, she recognizes that she need no longer remain with him as a reluctantly faithful wife and leaves the room to prepare to leave home and husband entirely. She soon returns, dressed for the street, even wearing "a black veil over her face" (p. 254). That veil perfectly objectifies the continuing inability of either Verloc to see the other.[26] But the characteristic mutual imperceptiveness that was previously the basis of their union combined with the consequent tragedy of Stevie's death soon ends that union. Verloc thinks that Winnie is going to her mother to complain of his recent actions. Because the hour is late and her emotional turmoil excessive, he would restrain her. She thinks that, since Stevie is dead, Verloc now wants "to keep her for nothing. And on this characteristic reasoning, having all the force of insane logic, Mrs. Verloc's disconnected wits went to work practically'' (p. 256).

Conrad demonstrates that Winnie is as wrong about her husband's immediate intentions as she was about his long-range plans for Stevie. He, quite reasonably, simply does not want his obviously distraught wife to go out so late at night. We have already been shown something about the disordered workings of Winnie's mind. But the essential nature of Mrs. Verloc's "insane logic" is further illustrated by the covert manner in which she projects her own shortcomings onto her husband. She would have it that he is the one who offered a secret bargain, who agreed to support Stevie as long as she remained with him, and who now threatens to keep something to which this transaction does not entitle him. Her husband, however, made no such deal. It is Mrs. Verloc, Conrad attests, who was "capable of a bargain the mere suspicion of which would have been infinitely shocking to Mr. Verloc's idea of love" (p. 259). Her bargain, made with herself, was to live with Verloc in order to take care of Stevie. Now that Stevie is dead, must she either remain with the man who is nothing to her or, by leaving him, admit that the marriage was empty and that her motives for entering it were largely mercenary? But there is one other alternative. She can claim to herself that Verloc has taken advantage of her situation, as of Stevie's. Her bargain therefore becomes "his," and, even worse, he forced it on her.

It is important to notice this projective element in Winnie's thinking because, immediately following such thoughts, Verloc utters the statements that most bring her to kill him. He observes, "it's as much your doing as mine," and then, even more explicitly, "if you will have it that I killed the boy, then you've killed him as much as I" (pp. 257-58). What he says is essentially valid. Even if he deliberately murdered Stevie, Winnie is still implicated. Since she picked Verloc as their support, the "murder" would be final proof of her mistaken judgment. And if the death were accidental, then Winnie is even more involved.[27] As Verloc himself points out, she "kept on shoving him [Stevie] in my way when I was half distracted with the worry of keeping the lot of us out of trouble. What the devil made you? One would think you were doing it on purpose" (p. 257). It is part of Conrad's overriding irony that she was.

Winnie had already found some reason to believe Verloc deliberately killed Stevie. Because her questionable innocence is here being questioned and because she tends to project blame onto others, she now has even more reason to do so. One final illusion, the vision of her brother exploding — "smashed branches, torn leaves, gravel, bits of brotherly flesh and bone, all spouting up together in the manner of a firework" (p. 260) — brings her to explode too. Her husband calls to her in "the note of wooing." But his invitation is not necessarily an invitation to intercourse. Verloc assumes his wife's silence shows that she is now calmer, that reconciliation is possible. And even if it is sex he has in mind, the physical union would simply attest that the marital union is still firmly established, that "all is forgiven." For Winnie, however, no reconciliation is possible. The bargain must end and it must end more decisively than by her merely departing. Conrad makes it quite clear that she could have done so. But it is equally clear that she insists on fallaciously believing that her husband must be completely responsible for Stevie's death and that she, like the boy, is his victim. "Retaliating," she kills him.

The manner in which the killing is described is consistent with the motives postulated. We do not see Winnie as "still defending Stevie" or executing "avenging retribution," and neither does she mystically become Stevie in any transcendent sense.[28] The text reads: "the resemblance of her face with that of her brother grew at every step, even to the droop of the lower lip, even to the slight divergence of the eyes" (p. 262). If the now homeless soul of Stevie enters his sister's breast, he turns her not into Stevie, the compassionate sympathizer with the suffering of the world, but into Stevie, the idiot.[29] The description emphasizes the drooping lower lip and unfocused eyes of the mentally deficient. Winnie's act also associates her with another less admirable quality of her brother. Like Stevie, she too can turn vicious in the presence of real or imagined suffering and injury. Conrad emphasizes both tendencies when he has Verloc recognize that "his wife had gone raving mad — murdering mad" and that he must participate in a "ghastly struggle with that armed lunatic" (p. 262).

Although Winnie kills her husband, she does not in any significant sense differentiate herself from him. In the house of the Verlocs "decorum had remained undisturbed" and "respectability was continued in immobility and silence" (p. 264). She and Verloc, a parody of a marriage before the murder, continue that parody despite his recent demise. "Except for the fact that Mrs. Verloc breathed these two would have been perfectly in accord" (p. 263). Since both are essentially moribund, "dead" to most of life, to each other, and to themselves, Verloc's actual death causes little change, and Winnie can resemble her husband murdered to approximately the same degree that she resembled him living. Earlier, their accord was equally perfect and resulted from the fact that both "refrained from going to the bottom of facts and motives" (p. 245). It is, of course, most ironic that what underlies this earlier accord, their willingness not to know each other, also underlies their final catastrophe.

Winnie resembles both her brother and her husband. She is, moreover, associated with these two in that she exhibits precisely the same qualities that contributed largely to the death of each. It is not then surprising that she dies too and dies in a fashion that partially duplicates the two earlier deaths. She is, first, as lost in London as her brother ever was. When Verloc's ticking blood becomes a trickle in which she sees her own time running out, Winnie flees the shop, intent on committing suicide by drowning. Wandering in the night, she soon realizes that she will not find a bridge before morning, but will herself be found "knocking about the streets" (p. 270). Unable to find even the Thames River (which is surely the city's most prominent landmark), she nevertheless decides to flee the country. Stevie could hardly be more irrational. Lost in this fashion, Winnie encounters Ossipon and is as unable to comprehend the way in which he plans to make use of her for his material advantage as Stevie was unable to fathom how the good Mr. Verloc was utilizing him.

In trusting Comrade Ossipon, she also has, as Leavis observes, her own "turn . . . to suppose herself loved for her own sake."[30] Winnie participates, in fact, in an extended scene that reenacts much of what went on in the preceding scene with her husband, except that she is now the suppliant, the chief victim of the extensive misunderstandings, and the one finally betrayed. Once more, although circumstances have altered, nothing has really changed. In short, Winnie and Ossipon, as much as Verloc and Winnie, illustrate the persistent pattern of two characters conversing but unable to communicate in any real sense with each other. The prospective lovers are no more in touch with each other's feelings than were the husband and wife.

Ossipon is certain that Verloc died in the explosion. Winnie is, for him, a woman recently widowed whose acquaintance might be profitably cultivated. Winnie, however, is looking for rescue and at once decides that Ossipon understands her hints about the failings of her late husband and sympathizes with her as an abused victim who has taken vengeance on "a devil" (p. 276). But for Ossipon her oblique comments merely refer to the late Verloc's possible sexual peccadilloes.

Ossipon's first awakening takes place when he and Winnie return to the shop and Winnie sends him in to put out the forgotten parlor light. Proceeding to do so, he comes upon Verloc "reposing quietly on the sofa" (p. 284). Instead of extinguishing the light, he experiences an immediate illumination. Obviously Verloc was not blown up in the park. Confronting the indubitable proof of his previous small miscalcuation, Ossipon suspects that this same evidence might also prove a much larger present mistake. Just when his affair with the Widow Verloc seemed to be progressing so smoothly, he suddenly finds himself in a situation that must be "madness, a nightmare, or a trap" (p. 284). He begins to recognize the world in which he is operating, a recognition that is carried further when he observes the manner in which Verloc has been murdered. He retches.

Precisely at this point, Winnie, afraid that a passing policeman might see her, enters the room and seizes Ossipon in a sudden embrace. Terrified, she wants him to shield her, to stand between her and the law, her and hanging. Terrified, he wants to escape from her arms, to flee from the scene so redolent of the recent crime. The two of them reenact the physical struggle that took place when Verloc earlier tried to prevent Winnie from leaving. On another level, however, this struggle is even more suggestive. While the policeman tries the door, the two inside stand "motionless, panting, breast to breast" (p. 287). Conrad here portrays a parody of a sexual embrace in which the male, the subject of Winnie's earlier illusion, strives not for union, but for separation, and in which the female asks not for the brief escape of a metaphoric death, but for the final escape of a real one: "If he comes in kill me — kill me, Tom" (p. 287).

The fullest indication of their misunderstanding one another comes, however, when Ossipon, at the railway station, observes that her brother was a perfect type. He meant that Stevie was a perfect example of one variety of a Lombrosian degenerate. But Winnie answers: "You took a lot of notice of him, Tom, I loved you for it" (p. 297). Such exchanges illustrate how Winnie can regard Ossipon as her savior, even while he sees her as an inhuman danger threatening his very existence. She is as mistaken about Ossipon as Verloc was about her. The same unconscious irony that characterized her husband's statements before she killed him also inform her comments to Ossipon. Confessing, for example, her inability to kill herself after Stevie's death, she says: "I suppose the cup of horrors was not full enough for such as me. Then when you came...." She does not complete the statement but adds, "I will live all my days for you, Tom!" (p. 298). And immediately Tom deserts. She is left alone, without money, ticketed for France. She too must face an awakening into a world of madness or nightmare, a world in which she has been, not in fancy but in fact, completely betrayed. Her cup of horrors, as her subsequent suicide proves, is finally full enough.

Conrad also demonstrates that Ossipon sees, in the unexpected events of an eventful evening, something of the horrors of his life too. After deserting Winnie, he walks endlessly through the London night. The second time he crosses a bridge, he stands for a long time looking down into "a black silence" (p. 300). But when he resumes his pointless wandering through "the enormous town slumbering monstrously on a carpet of mud under a veil of raw mist" (p. 300), he has apparently decided to substitute the deadness of total exhaustion for the death of suicide. That conveniently revised plan of escape is not completely successful. After his wanderings, Ossipon still sits for hours, motionless in his room. Only when the late afternoon sun shines in on him can he at last go to sleep. It is as if he needed some hint of some warmth somewhere.

A less capable novelist might well have ended the book with this seemingly conclusive scene. Ossipon would have been the last link in a chain of betrayals, a link that has come to recognize something of the nature of the chain and has found such knowledge crushing.[31] But Conrad, in his last chapter (suggestively, chapter thirteen), achieves patterns that resonate with larger thematic implications. He has already suggested, through the resolution of the Verloc's situation, how much private life is governed by illusions and delusions. His final chapter implies that all society, an age itself, can be equally irrational.

One movement in the last chapter is the further decline of Comrade Ossipon. That robust anarchist, whose thoughts hitherto were largely materialistic, is going to pieces, but not just from his awareness of how he came by his recently acquired money. He could partially undo that action and tries to do so by offering "the legacy" to the Professor. The "even tenor" of Ossipon's "revolutionary life" has been disastrously upset for deeper reasons, and he abandons the solace and support previously provided by his easy amorous successes for the more deadening solace of drink. Ossipon is haunted by what he thinks he knows. The newspaper article, "Suicide of Lady Passenger from a cross-Channel Boat," concludes: "*an impenetrable mystery seems destined to hang forever over this act of madness or despair*" (p. 307). These words, particularly the words "mystery," "madness," and "despair," reverberate loudly inside him. He believes he has experienced, both first-hand and second, something of the same madness and despair. But the words also reverberate because, like other of Conrad's representatives of modern materialistic man, Ossipon is hollow at the core. He is haunted by "the cursed knowledge" he can "never get rid of" (p. 307). And he is even more haunted by his scientific suspicion as to what the first haunting might mean.

All of the characters in *The Secret Agent* live in a grossly imperfect world, in an insane world that they do not understand and in which they are, in one way or another, victims of their ignorance. Because the world is incomprehensible, all characters also live largely by illusions and can be as much victims of their own particular imperfect view of reality as they are victims of life itself. In this context, Ossipon is especially exemplary. He is the man who *believes* in science, who invokes Lombroso "as an Italian peasant recommends himself to his favorite saint" (p. 297). Indeed, Ossipon's modern faith underlies the plot on which the whole novel turns. As the reader should recall, the planned outrage directed against Greenwich Observatory derives from Vladimir's observation that "the sacrosanct fetish of to-day is science" (p. 31). But Ossipon's science does not save him. This scientific materialist, who is "scientifically afraid of insanity" (p. 307), finds his fears self-fulfilling and becomes another victim, like the Verlocs, of the "fetish" of science. His decline is seen as evidence and proof of further decline, a process that will naturally continue beyond the end of the novel. When we last see Ossipon, "already he bowed his broad shoulders, his head of ambrosial locks, as if ready to receive the leather yoke of the sandwich board" (p. 311). And a man reduced to a walking billboard hardly demonstrates the advantages of possessing new or better information about the world through which he perambulates.

Ossipon is not, then, merely the last link in a chain of betrayals. At the end of the novel he is portrayed not in some final state, but in terms of what he must become. Conrad has so carefully contrived this part of his conclusion that his artistry in doing so has often gone unnoticed and has even been dubiously criticized. For example, as astute a critic as E.M.W. Tillyard could overlook the complex causes of Ossipon's "degeneration" and simply doubt that he "would have been haunted permanently by the thoughts of Mrs. Verloc's death and permanently put off his amorous adventures."[32] Tillyard suspects that Conrad here sacrifices psychological probability to plot demands, which is precisely what he avoids doing.

But the final fate of Ossipon is, as already suggested, important in still another way. Ossipon, materialistically devoted to science and justifying his shallowness in terms of that belief, suggests something of a larger world in which science is the main "fetish of the day." Times, like individuals, the novel implies, can have their special illusions. A particular age can be largely characterized by its particular illusion. These illusions can be as misleading for an age as for an individual. Such possibilities raise uncomfortable questions for anyone who, in late nineteenth-century fashion, trusts in the inevitability of a science-fostered progress or who, in twentieth-century fashion, expects still better science to cure those human ills largely created by an earlier, cruder, and more materialistic science. "Ossipon's harrowing mental torment" can be seen as appropriate, Thomas Gilmore observes, "if we realize how inhuman his science, his habit of scientific explanation or analysis, has made him."[33] A whole age can be similarly dehumanized, similarly harrowed. Seen from this perspective, Conrad's portrayal of Ossipon at the conclusion of the novel is radically open-ended.

Ossipon, however, is not the main character in the last chapter. It is the Professor, the "Perfect Anarchist," who most presides over the ending of *The Secret Agent*, a book which portrays an anarchic world. The very fact that the Professor is still present at the end of the novel shows something of that anarchy. Although Inspector Heat is fully aware of the Professor's home industry, he would rather not face the implications of such knowledge and so advances a convenient hypothesis about the possible guilt of Michaelis. He claims he "would deal with the devil himself, and take the consequences" (p. 132). Yet he clearly prefers not to deal with the Professor. Conrad thus demonstrates that even the upholders of law and order can be as willfully and self-advantageously blind to the dictates of legality as are the anarchists themselves.[34] They all — statesmen, policemen, tradesmen, and anarchists — come from the same basket. Their world is, in fact, so disordered that conservative anarchists can, in a wildly irrational society, still talk of overthrowing order.[35]

There is no order to overthrow. The ending of the novel, despite the claims of various critics, does not suggest the presence of any higher order or the workings of any ultimate justice.[36] Verloc does not die to pay for his crime against Stevie nor does he die as punishment for his illusions. Killing her husband does not drive Winnie to kill herself. And if justice is not served by either the homicide or the suicide, it fares even worse with Vladimir and with the Professor. One provided the plot and the other supplied the bomb that resulted in the first death. Verloc is, in one sense, merely the secret agent who acts for those who are most reactionary or most revolutionary. His trial could have brought to light the reasons for the bombing and the source of the bomb. The Assistant Commissioner might have controlled Vladimir; Inspector Heat might have been forced to cope with the Professor. But no trial takes place. Both men, one representing the anarchy of blindly reactionary politics and the other the anarchy of blinding revolutionary politics, are still free at the end of the novel.

No one, however, triumphs, and especially not the Professor. He lives in a "poverty suggesting the starvation of every human need except mere bread" (p. 302). He mocks Michaelis's vision of the world as one immense hospital in which the strong will care for the weak and defends his own vision of the strong exterminating the weak until "every taint, every vice, every prejudice, every convention" has met "its doom" (p. 303). He might himself then remain if he were strong enough. But while so arguing, his "large ears, thin like membranes, and standing far out from the sides of his frail skull," blush deep red at the idea of such envisioned strength (p. 304). Both the ears and the blush testify to the illusory nature of his thought. If "only the *Übermenschen* shall inherit the earth, then surely he shall be the first to be exterminated."[37] The Professor, moreover, can calmly toast "the destruction of what is" (p. 306), despite his "astounding ignorance of worldly conditions" (p. 80). And he is equally ignorant of himself. He does not recognize that he is merely the fanatic son of a fanatic father (with one fanaticism merely substituted for another, he does not himself embody much of a revolution) nor does he recognize how much his theory and his actions derive from a perverted sexuality. With his hand deep in "the left pocket of his trousers, grasping lightly the india-rubber ball, the supreme guarantee of his sinister freedom" (p. 81), he continually, as Joseph Fradin observes, anticipates his own ultimate climax. This would turn him, like Stevie, into a heap of fragments and so render even him more (alteration without real change) an "analogue of the broken lives in the morally anarchic city."[38]

His explosion would really change nothing nor would it render him the transcendent being he claims to be. As Jacques Darras rightly observes, the Professor "cannot incarnate himself without being disincarnated."[39] The most he can do is to make another little hole in time, for men are too many and time does not stop and bombs (at least then) were not big enough. The central action in the book is, from this point of view, completely futile. The attack on Greenwich Observatory can symbolize, as R.W. Stallman maintains, the desire to destroy all time.[40] But both the total failure of the attack and the general treatment of time in the novel show, as David Kubal points out, the senselessness of such an attack.[41] Man cannot manage his own world. How can he control time within that world, much less abolish it?[42] The Perfect Anarchist, who wishes to create a chaotic new world free from process and time, laments, at the end of the novel, that madness and despair are no more. Time has taken away all the passions he might use to move the world. But madness and despair, as the novel amply demonstrates, definitely remain. The mad (in any conventional sense) Professor might possibly recognize his own madness and, in his lamentation, he is, in fact, despairing. The Professor, like all men, is time's victim but not in the sense he believes. He too lives by illusions and cannot alter, much less master, either time or his world.

The Professor does not know the world, and the world returns the compliment. He walks, as described in the last sentence of the novel, through the "odious multitude of mankind." While "his thoughts caressed the images of ruin and destruction," the Professor "passed on unsuspected and deadly, like a pest in the street full of men" (p. 311). It is difficult to believe with Sister Jane Marie Luecke that a street full of men makes this ending affirmative.[43] The novel has shown too clearly how all men, through ignorance and necessary illusions, are victims. Some might even be victims of the Professor's ultimate blast. He, like much else in life, is unsuspected. But he is deadly and he is, inescapably, there. His presence, in fact, completes another pattern in the novel. Stevie was an incompetent with a bomb; Winnie was a madwoman with a knife. The Professor remains, at the conclusion of the novel, more deranged and dangerous than either.

His final condition, like Ossipon's, is open-ended. Conrad leaves us, as Norman N. Holland observes, "with the persistent question of the Professor 'unsuspected and deadly.' "[44] And the questions inherent in the Professor are considerably more unsettling than those that center on Ossipon. What the Perfect Anarchist represents is irrational man committed to irrational destruction in an irrational world, one in which the "authorities" cannot even logically number the houses on a street but are nevertheless unwilling to recognize the irrational. The presence of the Professor reverberates, moreover, beyond the end of the novel and beyond the time of the novel. "If Conrad's portrayal in *Nostromo* of material progress has a remarkably prophetic quality, so too does his sense of what men like the Professor would be capable of in the way of progress!"[45]

We are left, then, at the end of *The Secret Agent* with the same problems that pervade the novel, the illusions and delusions, the madness and despair that are inescapable in an irrational world. The book must exhibit open form. Such problems, by their very nature, cannot be resolved by any ending short of death, and even then they are not solved but only suspended. Conrad, as Joseph I. Fradin points out, demonstrates that life itself, like the bell which, at the beginning of the novel, summons the Verlocs, "is irreparably cracked."[46]

The best that any character can achieve is to counter the absurdity of existence with some equally absord palliative. Even the relatively capable Assistant Commissioner needs the sense of order that his whist supplies and he depends on this as if it were a drug. Inspector Heat has his trusted racing sheet; Sir Ethelred has his vision of nationalizing the fisheries; the great lady has her pet anarchist; the various anarchists have their various hypothetical futures; the Professor has, finally, his bomb.

4

Deluded Vision in *Under Western Eyes*

Under Western Eyes does not profit from its place in the Conrad canon. Coming after *Lord Jim, Nostromo,* and *The Secret Agent,* it is often criticized for not measuring up to the high standards established by the three preceding masterpieces and thereby condemned as one of its author's less successful artistic achievements. Albert Guerard, for example, finds this particular book comparatively conventional. Art, he argues, "does not to the same degree stand between the reader and the material to control that reader's response" in *Under Western Eyes* as it does in other Conrad works. Compared to an "art novel" such as *Lord Jim*, the later novel is, for this critic, definitely "the less original of the two."[1]

But if the book as a whole seems to be, for a Conrad novel, uncommonly undistinguished, its conclusion can seem even more so. Consider especially the final scene which takes place some two years after the main events described in *Under Western Eyes.* The narrator, an elderly English professor of languages, conveniently encounters Sophia Antonovna who tells him how both Natalia and Razumov live now that they have left Geneva and returned permanently to Russia. Not only are the main characters thus disposed of, the narrator, through this final conversation, also learns of what ultimately happened to less important characters like Nikita and Peter Ivanovitch. Such an ending does seem epiloguish and distinctly old-fashioned, an impression which has prompted extended condemnation of the conclusion to the novel. Thus Frederick Karl argues that Conrad's attempt to "account for everyone while tying together all loose ends" necessarily "lacks proportion and fails to make sense dramatically."[2] The whole final section of the novel represents, for Karl, an artistic failure. The author "seriously misjudged the true climax of his story"; he should have ended the novel with "Razumov's confession to Miss Haldin."[3]

But neither Guerard nor Karl, I would argue, does justice to the artistic subtlety which Conrad exhibits in *Under Western Eyes.* The novel should be assessed according to its own terms and not through comparisons with earlier Conrad successes— complex works which make for rather unmanageable touchstones. Furthermore, any such touchstones are not really required, for

Conrad makes the "terms" of the novel quite clear in the book itself, particularly in its ending. In fact, even while criticizing the conclusion of *Under Western Eyes* as crudely contrived, Karl overlooks the full complexity of what he condemns, and some of his specific strictures seem particularly shortsighted. John Hagan, for example, shows that Razumov's confession to seemingly ridiculous revolutionaries is not, as Karl claims, "meaningless."[4] A study of Conrad's sources and a consequent familiarity with the career of Evno Azoff should have kept this same critic from insisting "it is incredible that in the meeting between Mikulin and Peter Ivanovitch the former should divulge Nikita's true identity."[5] As Avrom Fleishman notes, "A.A. Lopuchin, a chief of the Ochrana, similarly revealed the policy spy Evno Azoff to the revolutionary leader Vladimir Burtsev while they were thrown together by chance on a German train."[6] Nor is it, as Karl maintains, "impossible to believe" that Sophia Antonovna would visit Razumov after his second confession in which he admits to the revolutionaries that he informed on Haldin and subsequently spied on them.[7] Sophia Antonovna, the most discerning and capable revolutionary in the book, insists, in her final conversation with the narrator, that Razumov's confessions showed "character." She visits him because he confessed. There is, therefore, no real occasion for incredulity even though the narrator is astonished. "His astonishment," as Guerard rightly observes, mostly reflects "his own automatic moralism."[8]

Karl, however, is particularly questionable when he views the conclusion of the novel as Conrad's attempt to resolve fully all the issues of the book and thus provide a traditional closed ending. Other critics continue to find *Under Western Eyes* distinctly unclosed. Penn Szittya, for example, notes that the text provides "not a message but an experience of baffling duplicity and duality in the medium itself."[9] And in another recent essay, "Secrets and Narrative Sequence," Frank Kermode magisterially demonstrates how the unfolding ordered novel blatantly hides other chaotic readings of itself: "it gives the western eye its box, its civilized mediocrity, but keeps its secrets also. . . . And the text, almost with 'cynicism,' tells us what is there, confident that we shall ignore it."[10] Indeed, even in the simple declarative sentence with which the novel concludes there is more than meets the narrator's — or the casual reader's — eye. The old professor voices an "impious hope" that Peter Ivanovitch might be beaten by his peasant wife. With a "firm voice," Sophia Antonovna answers, "Peter Ivanovitch is an inspired man."[11]

Her claim, Jocelyn Baines suggests, must be seen as "superbly ironic."[12] Yet the full import of such irony has not been assessed. Essentially, Peter Ivanovitch *is not* an inspired man. Conrad, in his "Author's Note," classifies this particular revolutionary and Madame de S. together as "apes of a sinister jungle" who "are treated as their grimaces deserve" (p. ix). In the novel itself, he exposes "the great feminist" as a self-serving sham. Peter Ivanovitch's treatment of Tekla belies his pretended solicitude for women and proves him a complete hypocrite. Supposedly a revolutionary leader, he has no real sympathy for those whose suffering might justify some social upheaval and, in semantic self-contradiction, insists that his revolution will keep the dregs of society at the bottom. Moreover, his marriage, an attempt to seek happiness in private life, indicates that Peter Ivanovitch finally abandons cause, comrades, and the public objectives of the revolution. "And all for the sake of a peasant girl" (p. 382). Yet Sophia Antonovna, although she is an intelligent and capable woman, still admires this personally ambitious bourgeois romantic. A real revolutionary radically misestimates the qualities of a supposed revolutionary, and therein lies one of Conrad's little ironies. Since the essential events of the novel derive from Haldin's delusion regarding Razumov, the book begins and ends with the same basic situation. But there is a difference between the first mistake and the final one. Haldin misjudges Razumov with tragic consequences for them both. When Sophia Antonovna misjudges Peter Ivanovitch neither suffers. Error is ever present; the consequences of error are, however, arbitrary, capricious, even absurd.

Sophia Antonovna is not the only one deluded at the end of the novel. Told of Nikita's double treachery, the professor of languages responds, "I had a glimpse of that brute.... How any of you could have been deceived for half a day passes my comprehension!" (p. 380). But the one here deceived is mostly the narrator. His statement implies that, with a single glance, he can fathom the nature of another man. Individuals must be what they seem to be; a man's outward appearance necessarily attests to his inner reality. Of course the professor's own experience should have taught him otherwise. For example, throughout the early sections of the novel he is concerned with the problem of protecting Natalia from the great danger posed, so he believes, by the inhabitants of the Chateau Borel. As Claire Rosenfield notes, he thus totally overlooks the real danger that menaced the girl.[13] Peter Ivanovitch's desire for still another disciple represents a very minor threat when compared to Razumov's wish to revenge himself on Haldin by stealing Natalia's soul. Furthermore, long before he makes his statement regarding Nikita, the narrator knows that he has been mistaken about Razumov. When he reads the latter's letter to Natalia, he sees how his own well-meant insistence that the "friend" of the brother should befriend the sister actually affected that intended second protector. Razumov wrote: "The old man you introduced me to insisted on walking with me. I don't know who he is. He talked of you, of your lonely, helpless state, and every word of that friend of yours was egging me on to the unpardonable sin of stealing a soul. Could he have been the devil himself in the shape of an old Englishman?" (pp. 359-60). Yet this same "old Englishman" can later believe that Nikita's essential duplicity should be immediately obvious to any discerning observer — anyone such as himself. Complacently assured of his own perspicacity, he remains as mistaken about himself as Sophia Antonovna is about Peter Ivanovitch.

Illusion, in *Under Western Eyes*, seems ubiquitous, inescapable. It is not just one particular scene but the whole novel which illustrates "the invincible nature of human error" and partly plumbs "the utmost depths of self-deception" (p. 282). The narrator, for example, voicing these statements in reference to Sophia Antonovna's inability to fathom the truth about Razumov during the course of a lengthy interview, implies that he would have been more discerning. Yet, as just noted, he fared no better, for he too seriously misjudged the same individual. Similarly, referring to the revolutionaries' failure to appreciate Tekla's "irresistible vocation" as "a good Samaritan," he later observes, "there is not much perspicacity in the world" (p. 374). But he immediately "regretted that observation." Since it was addressed to Natalia Haldin who has just discovered how mistaken she was about Razumov, supposedly her brother's closest friend, the professor realizes that he has spoken most tactlessly. He is, nevertheless, still quite right. There is, in the novel, "not much perspicacity." And he is, at the time, most imperceptive to say so.

The theme of illusion, however, finds its chief focus in the character of Razumov. This young Russian's name — significantly an *assumed* name— derives from a Russian and Polish verb, *razumet*, meaning, in both languages, "to reason." By occupation he is, ironically, a student of philosophy. Yet he is continually misjudged and misjudging. Briefly, Haldin and his fellow student revolutionaries view Razumov as a sternly dedicated foe of a reactionary government. That same government perceived in Razumov a fortuitous opportunity to recruit a secret agent. According to their view, he is a confirmed patriot and should serve to support the status quo. Razumov, however, sees himself as one who modestly aspires to be merely "a celebrated old professor, decorated, possibly a Privy Councillor, one of the glories of Russia — nothing more" (p. 13). But all three views prove fallacious. Razumov is not a revolutionary, not a reactionary, nor is he, as he prefers to believe, a likely candidate for future fame.

Conrad, in fact, manipulates the events of the novel so that the manner in which others are deceived about Razumov finally forces him to see that he was also most deceived about himself. This process begins with Haldin's mistake, which precipitates a disastrous personal crisis in the life of the other young student and presents him with continuing dilemmas he is incapable of resolving. As Razumov finally recognizes, "the Revolution had sought him out to put to a sudden test his dormant instincts, his half-conscious thoughts and almost wholly unconscious ambitions" (p. 294). Moreover, the examination is not at all a fair one. It is a cruelly ironic parody of a test in that what is tested — Razumov's instincts, thoughts, and ambitions (his desire to achieve some place in his society) — must be denied if he is to pass the test. Yet if he passes the test he, of course, fails himself. His immediate reaction to Haldin's visit is not therefore surprising. As soon as he was caught in the impossible dilemma of having to align his "willed" and "determined future" with either "the lawlessness of autocracy" or "the lawlessness of revolution," Razumov "had a distinct sensation of his very existence being undermined in some mysterious manner, of his moral supports falling away from him one by one" (pp. 76-77). He is ultimately forced to realize that he can achieve no kind of renown, that he "had neither the simplicity nor the courage nor the self-possession to be a scoundrel, or an exceptionally able man" (p. 362).

This statement should not suggest a simple dichotomy between "scoundrel" and "exceptionally able man." Razumov himself immediately blurs any absolute distinction by bitterly asking if anyone in Russia can tell the difference. As his own experience teaches, the two apparent opposites can easily coalesce. He aspired to an honored position. Hard work and concise thought should give him what he was born without, a definite identity. Thus, as the novel begins, he intends to write an essay that must win the silver medal — a first step towards and perfect symbol of his intended success. But, returning to his apartment to commence work on the essay, to begin the actual process which "would convert the label Razumov into an honored name," he is "horribly startled" to find "a strange figure" standing "all black . . . in the dusk" (p. 14). Haldin has intruded, into Razumov's room and into his life.

Because he is not certain of his own sympathies (neither a complete revolutionary nor a confirmed reactionary), there is no clear course of action immediately open to Razumov. That state of affairs soon becomes the basic pattern of his experience. As George Goodin points out: "The choices available to Razumov come in the form of dilemmas. Over and over, he is offered alternatives, neither one of which he really wants."[14] Yet he must choose. And again his first impossible quandary is indicative of what is to come. "Considering the myopic zeal of both autocratic state and revolutionaries," the "situation" effected by Haldin's visit, Bruce Johnson convincingly argues, "does not admit of neutrality; inaction will be interpreted as action and neutrality will seem hostile to both sides."[15] Razumov must, moreover, immediately determine what course of action he will pursue. If he is going to do his "patriotic" duty — and his desire that he gain social status through some successful public career certainly aligns him with society and against the revolution — he must do so at once. Any delay, if discovered, will compromise him in the eyes of the authorities and seriously jeopardize the future he has planned. But going at once to the police also involves a definite danger. Why should they believe that Haldin's expectations were unfounded? There is, in short, no way in which those qualities that were to bring Razumov honor can serve him in this particular dilemma. In fact, the more he rationally assesses his situation, the more he realizes that he cannot escape acting, in some sense, as a scoundrel. His plan was to win public honor, but because he cannot be true both to his own convictions and to Haldin's misplaced trust, he must, in some sense, privately debase himself.[16]

Conrad's irony soon becomes more complex. When Razumov solves his first quandary by siding with the authorities, his solution soon precipitates a far more perplexing problem than the one which it was intended to resolve. Informing on Haldin brings Razumov to the attention of his government. When that government decides to employ him to infiltrate foreign-based revolutionary movements, he must become what he planned to be, a public servant, but not in the sense he intended. He will act far more privately than any "Privy Councillor." Ironically, the student who aspired to be part of the superstructure of the social edifice finds himself forced to serve as one of its most hidden underpinnings. Moreover, the more capably he serves, the more he dishonors himself in his own eyes. As a secret agent, he deliberately does to others what Haldin unintentionally did to him; he makes those on whom he spies victims of a misplaced trust. Again capability and rascality converge and force this obscure would-be conqueror of fame to condemn in himself the precise quality that should have brought him victory. No wonder Razumov exhibits such ironic bitterness — an emotion that surely derives from more than his fear of being discovered — throughout the middle sections of the novel.

He desired to achieve renown and believed he possessed the qualities — intelligence and dedication — necessary to do so. Yet Conrad shows that, even as Razumov attempts to cope with the impossible dilemmas that are forced upon him, he must increasingly perceive the degree to which he is dishonoring himself. His rationality thus serves to reveal the extent of his failure. He is not earning the renown that he sought nor is he living according to his tenuous conception of his own identity. Early in the novel, caught in a situation he could not master, Razumov insisted that, if he must be a reed, he would at least be "a thinking reed" (p. 89).[17] Later he apparently reaches a similar decision. If he must be a rogue, he will be a thinking rogue. He will prove that he is still superior to others by precipitating and manipulating in them a "villainy" cruder than his own. They will be scoundrels too, but stupid scoundrels. That is why Razumov requires the impulsive Kostia to steal from his own father money that is thereupon callously thrown away. Razumov did not need these funds. Instead, he wished to prove (mainly to himself) that Kostia was in no way his moral superior and definitely was his intellectual inferior. Yet this reassurance must be singularly unsatisfying, for Razumov only further demeans himself with such attempts to prove his relative superiority.

Razumov has, therefore, a certain justification when he claims, in his final letter to Nathalie, "Victor Haldin had stolen the truth of my life from me, who had nothing else in the world, and he boasted of living on through you on this earth where I had no place to lay my head" (p. 359). Such a theft cannot be extenuated by arguing, as does Christopher Cooper, that Haldin is justified in involving an unwilling accomplice because "he is of the firm conviction that Razumov is a fellow conspirator, who would therefore be more than eager to help him"[18] Haldin's "firm conviction" is better described as a gratuitous assumption, and as such indicates the pervasiveness of misjudgment throughout the novel. There is no evidence at all for Haldin positing as a "co-conspirator" this man with whom, to say the least, he has never conspired. As John Hagan rightly observes, "by a bitterly cruel irony, Razumov's aloofness from the revolutionary students is the very thing which wins him the fatal reputation of being worthy of their confidence."[19] Under these circumstances, Razumov can hardly be held responsible for another's unsolicited trust.

Haldin himself singularly fails in his attempt to defend his act. "It occurred to me that you — you have no one belonging to you — no ties, no one to suffer for it if this came out by some means" (p. 19). The assumptions implicit in this assertion are callously crude. As Razumov sees, the very fact that he has little, no family or position, ostensibly justifies Haldin who jeopardizes what little he has, his lonely independence and his hope for future fame. That Haldin then justifies this justification by claiming he can speak openly "to a superior mind" only makes the whole rationalization that much less acceptable to the mind addressed.

Razumov at once imaginatively assesses a possible future made all too probable because of Haldin's mistake. "He saw himself deported by an administrative order, his life broken, ruined, and robbed of all hope. He saw himself — at best — leading a miserable existence under police supervision in some small, far-away provincial town" (p. 21). He also sees that, contrary to Haldin's claims, this possible fate is not made less severe by his present lonliness. "Others had fathers, mothers, brothers, relations, connexions, to move heaven and earth on their behalf — he had no one. The very officials that sentenced him some morning would forget his existence before sunset" (p. 21). Such considerations substantially justify his subsequent actions. Not surprisingly, Razumov's "fear gives way to rage, rage to hate."[20] He informs on Haldin and so assures the latter's capture and execution.

To punish Haldin for his presumption does not, however, reestablish the original tenor of Razumov's life, for his first dilemma, how to cope with an unwelcome intruder, is soon replaced by the more complex problem of reconciling his conception of himself with his new occupation as a police spy. Tony Tanner observes that Razumov's existence continues to be "a grotesque pantomime... a nightmare."[21] Haldin continues to haunt him, literally and figuratively, while Razumov continues to despise the man who has destroyed his plan of life and to plot further revenge against the destroyer. Razumov can do so because, before Haldin's arrest, Haldin did suggest that he would still survive in the person of his sister. What at first seemed another turn of the screw — an unintended taunt that further emphasized the contrast between Razumov as lonely and Haldin as loved — ironically serves to provide Razumov with a way of avenging himself on Haldin despite the latter's demise. When he meets Natalia and finds her, as her brother claimed, trusting and unsuspecting, he sees that the man he continues to despise need not live on in the person of the sister. Her life can be destroyed.

Several critics have nevertheless suggested that the plot against Natalia is not properly part of the novel. Guerard, for example, argues that Razumov, when he admits his designs against the girl, "claims to have been a much more cynical person, in his relationship with Nathalie Haldin, than we have had any reason to suspect."[22] The whole scheme, for Guerard, represents a possible carry-over from the more melodramatic novel Conrad originally planned to write. J.I.M. Stewart has also maintained that this episode represents Conrad reverting "to the conventions of melodrama which his first plan would have enforced upon him." Arguing that the plot to steal Nathalie's soul is gratuitously tacked on to the end of the novel, Stewart also complains that "we may turn back and search the novel in vain for any hint of the 'atrocious temptation.' "[23]

Implicit in both charges is the assumption that an episode inadequately foreshadowed must represent an artistic flaw. But by objecting to the element of surprise, Guerard and Stewart equally fail to see how the unexpected serves a definite artistic function. Conrad's narrative strategy requires that his narrator reveal such facts as he knows in roughly the same order in which those facts became known. Thus, during the middle sections of the novel, the reader is not told why Razumov came to Geneva even though the retrospective narrator, in the course of telling his tale, knows all along that the apparent revolutionary had really been recruited as a police spy. In the same fashion, the reader is not informed of the plot against Natalia. The result of this narrative strategy — and the justification for it — is to place before the reader the same essential problem that is faced by various characters in the novel. The reader, too, is invited to surmise, to construct theories as to Razumov and his intentions. Like Natalia and the narrator, we must, especially in the second and third part of the novel, rely on appearances — words and actions, expression and gesture — to understand Razumov. Again like Natalia and the narrator, the reader can also discover that appearances deceive. Considering the importance of illusions and delusions throughout the novel, the perceptive reader should, paradoxically, be surprised if he is not surprised. Yet, looking back, our surprise should not be that great either. Viewed retrospectively, consequences and causes clearly connect. So we have what might be termed postshadowing instead of foreshadowing. Large, crucial events point back to underlying motives instead of emerging from a character's obvious intentions and effort. And of course Razumov is not going to admit in advance his plan to steal the soul of Natalia

Haldin. But after he has acknowledged his failure and admitted his plot we can see that he saw Natalia as "Haldin's surviving image and in their first meeting . . . transferred his anger against Haldin to her."[24]

As the plot against Natalia unfolds in the novel, Natalia is deceived, the narrator is certainly deceived, and the reader is probably deceived too. There is also a fourth participant in this pervasive deception. Just as Razumov's plan to destroy that young woman's life represents his basest attempt to mislead another, it also represents his basest attempt to deceive himself. Consider, in this context, how he prompts himself to act by pretending a diabolical devotion to evil. Yet we simply cannot believe him when he writes retrospectively to Natalia and, referring to their first meeting, claims: "If you could have looked then into my heart, you would have cried aloud with terror and disgust" (p. 359). Supposedly practicing his profession as a spy, he must force himself to deceive even the sham revolutionaries he, not without reason, despises. And clearly, as his first confession proves, he cannot bring himself to carry out his plot against Natalia. In short, he is not at all what he sometimes claims to be, a Mephistophelian figure amorally capable of anything.

Nor is he, as he at other times unconvincingly rationalizes, a man simply seeking a crudely just vengeance. Razumov, as earlier noted, readily assumes that his life has been undone by Haldin's uninvited trust. Yet this comfortable claim — that another is mostly responsible for the chaos in his own life — is not ultimately tenable. He aspired to public renown and planned to achieve that end by becoming first a distinguished professor and finally a famous public servant, perhaps even the "great autocrat of the future" (p. 35). Conrad, however, makes it ironically evident that not all professors are distinguished, not all public servants famous. Razumov's own experiences should have shown him how jejune his original ambitions actually were. But he refuses to see that the society in which he was to win honor is itself not honorable, that the government he would gladly serve finds it more expedient merely to use him. Conrad also makes it quite clear that success on a higher level is not necessarily what Razumov dreamed it to be. Councillor Mikulin, for example, embodies one aspect of Razumov's aspirations.[25] As such, he proves that a high-placed government official is not necessarily renowned. This councillor was distinguished only among "his intimates" and only as "an enlightened patron of the art of female dancing" (p. 305). He is not "heard of" by "the larger world" until, paradoxically, he sinks from sight amidst the "stir of vaguely seen monstrosities" in a "mysterious disturbance of muddy waters" (p. 305). Mikulin's position brings him, finally, the infamy of this decline made more infamous by the fact that it was not deserved but was imposed by the same bureaucracy he capably served.

Mikulin, moreover, is not the only possible future personified for the protagonist in the novel. As Robert Secor observes, "the professor Razumov seeks to become is what the narrator already is."[26] The presence in the book of this obtuse old man, one who is pathetically isolated from the world around him and who consistently misjudges himself and his few associates, mocks Razumov's aspirations even more than does the career of Councillor Mikulin. Nevertheless, throughout most of the novel, Razumov blames his ruined hopes on Haldin's error instead of recognizing the foolishness of his own original ambitions.

There is, therefore, a two-fold purpose to Razumov's attempts to manipulate others. As earlier noted, if he must be a rogue he will be a thinking rogue and so salvage some of his pride. But this very desire to be a capable scoundrel can also represent a deeper attempt to convince himself that his original intentions were reasonable and that the pride he attempts to salvage is justifiable. In the face of considerable evidence to the contrary, he seems intent on demonstrating that, given the chance, he would have distinguished himself in a good cause just as well as he will distinguish himself in an evil one. He cannot, however, carry out the one major immoral task he set himself to accomplish.

Razumov intends to prove his capability for evil by destroying Natalia's life, an act which would also demonstrate how capably he can avenge the destruction of his own life. Yet his second plan, like his first one, is subverted by an unexpected presence. Razumov, as he leaves Mrs. Haldin after telling her the fortuitous story of Ziemianitch's supposed remorse and suicide, is perturbed by the way in which she did not believe his account, but he is still committed to his calculated revenge. The difficult interview has prompted a deeper awareness of how abidingly Haldin "continued to exist in the affection of that mourning old woman, in the thoughts of all these people posing for lovers of humanity" (p. 341). Although dead, Haldin still has a firm place in the world, whereas Razumov's own position is more tenuous than ever. Previously he had no real identity, now he has only a spurious one. Yet his spurious position at least seems secure. "Nothing could touch him now; in the eyes of the revolutionists there was no shadow on his past" (p. 340). Such was his thought as he again "walked over" Haldin's phantom and by telling his misleading story to "the phantom's mother" supposedly left that ghost "lying powerless and passive" behind him (p. 340).

His anticipated security is short-lived. Leaving the mother, he unexpectedly encounters the daughter. Natalia had been futilely seeking him through the streets of Geneva, desperate for him to come to her mother. As they meet, Natalia's relief matches his dismay. "Her presence in the ante-room was as unforeseen as the apparition of her brother had been" (p. 341), as unforeseen as Haldin's presence in Razumov's room. Paradoxically, this final encounter with his intended victim further prompts Razumov to recognize that he himself is his own chief victim and that his previously asserted confidence was most unwarranted. As he admits, his interview with Mrs. Haldin "troubled him like some strange discovery" (p. 340). Her refusal to accept his account of the manner in which her son died had already prompted Razumov to suspect that he is one "given up to destruction" (p. 341). He would flee this suspicion, but his flight immediately brings him to Natalia and an incomparably more difficult interview. In this interview, he is completely undone by one seemingly insignificant act. To show how openly and honestly she will talk with him, Natalia removes her veil.

Razumov at once discovers that he cannot repeat to the daughter the fiction he has imposed upon her mother. This discovery does not derive solely from a growing love for his prospective victim. For some time, Razumov's dawning love and Razumov's determined plot have been at odds with each other. The identity of the Natalia he desires and the Miss Haldin he intends to destroy is a matter that he has hitherto refused to consider. With one term or the other of this contradictory equation, Razumov, in some way, is necessarily deluding himself. Recognition comes with the removal of the veil. When he really sees Natalia, he also begins to perceive how much he has misled himself, how little he understood his own desires, and how he is the one he "betrayed most basely" (p. 361).

Essentially, he recognizes himself in her and Haldin in himself. That new double perspective demands that he acknowledge the nature of his plot and what adhering to it would indicate about his own confused nature. She will be, like him, a victim, even a "predestined victim" (p. 349). But can he really inflict on another the defeat he has suffered himself, especially when he knows how devastating that defeat is? And more to the point, must he become what he believes her brother to be — the despised undoer of another's life? He would be even worse than Haldin who merely mistakenly assumed a disastrous trust; he has calculatingly cultivated one in order to destroy it.

As he begins to see himself in this new light, Razumov perceives that the last largest step in a progressive degeneration would be entirely of his own making. He knows what the destruction of a life means through what Haldin and Councillor Mikulin have effected in his own existence. The former, anticipating an ally in his revolt against the Czarist government, brought Razumov to betray a bond that he had never accepted. The latter, conveniently employing a tool to forestall revolt, required Razumov to betray others who accepted a pretended bond. But neither man acted with the cold calculation that characterizes Razumov's projected attempt to destroy Natalia. In short, his plot makes him more despicable than Haldin, the man he most despises. He can neither inflict that low status on himself nor live with himself if he did. He therefore confesses, not to atone for informing on a careless and even (he can still think) contemptible revolutionary, but "to purge himself of the guilt of contriving the destruction of Nathalie."[27]

Razumov's confession to Natalia does not, however, presage any abatement of illusion. Conrad makes it quite clear that mistakes and misjudgments continue. Significantly, the whole confession scene is framed by the narrator's erroneous suppositions. The elderly professor first assumes that he knows what is about to transpire and even congratulates himself on his foresight: "I could not mistake the significance of this late visit. . . . The true cause dawned upon me: he had discovered that he needed her — and she was moved by the same feeling" (p. 347). But this reading of the meeting about to take place could not be more wide of the mark. Anticipating a tender love scene that would eternally unite the young Russians, the narrator witnesses instead the completely unexpected confession that forever severs them.

He is not chastened by that error. As the scene concludes, the old professor makes a second mistake which is merely the inversion of his previous one. He now imagines that he comprehends the significance of what he has just witnessed. "The meaning of what I had seen reached my mind with a staggering shock" — a meaning immediately elucidated for Miss Haldin: " 'That miserable wretch has carried off your veil!' I cried, in the scared, deadened voice of an awful discovery" (p. 356). With this evaluation ("probably the most strained remark ever uttered by a Conrad character"[28]), the narrator's obtuseness reaches monumental proportions. Blindly oblivious to the larger implications of Razumov's confession, his exaggerated horror derives from one minor act that he nevertheless views as an unforgivable breach of decorum. No gentleman would ever take any personal garment from a lady. Nathalie, however, is obviously not concerned with the minor matter of a purloined veil when she answers him: "It is impossible to be more unhappy. . . . It is impossible. . . . I feel my heart becoming like ice" (p. 356).

The narrator, throughout the conclusion of the novel, also insists on maintaining a more general illusion, one that he lets waver only once. When Natalia removes her veil and thus encourages Razumov to see through a metaphoric veil behind which he has hitherto hidden, the professor also feels a momentary impulse to discard one of his own pervasive pretenses. As "she raised her hands above her head to untie her veil," that action "displayed for an instant the seductive grace of her youthful figure" (p. 347). Shadowed by her hat rim, her eyes briefly "had an enticing lustre" (p. 348). Prompted by the romantic triumph he believes Razumov is about to achieve, the narrator momentarily sees Nathalie as a seductively desirable woman. But the danger soon passes. The professor will not recognize that he vicariously participates in Razumov's ostensible romance to protect himself from the problem of having to attend to his own or that he pretends to a safe relationship with the young lady as a substitute for a very different relationship, the possibility of which he will not permit himself to consider. Throughout most of the novel he seems, indeed, perversely determined to deprive Natalia of the female sexuality he here briefly perceives. Earlier, "her glance was as direct and trustful as that of a young man" (p. 102); her handshake expressed "a sort of exquisite virility" (p. 118); her voice was "fascinating with its masculine . . . quality" (p. 141). But even these ostensibly safe claims can still suggest dangerous feelings. The virility is exquisite; the masculine voice fascinates. The reader, therefore, need not unreservedly accept the professor's occasional proclamations that he is attached to Natalia only as a former teacher and a safely ancient friend.[29]

Perhaps because he earlier faltered, the narrator has, at the end of the novel, managed to make his pretense much more secure. He will be a disinterested friend, so disinterested that, as a friend, he can counsel perpetual separation. In his last encounter with Nathalie — a visit that begins on a safely mundane level: "we exchanged a few words about her health, mine" (p. 372) — she tells him that she has accepted his advice and will return permanently to Russia. The narrator notes: "It was all to be as I had wished it. And it was to be for life. We should never see each other again. Never!" And then, with crowning irony, Conrad has him add, "I gathered this success to my breast" (p. 373). He must be satisfied with that success, for he shall never embrace the girl. Intent on demonstrating that their relationship is totally respectable according to the sterile proprieties of Geneva, he shall never even see her again. Illusion, originally designed to make his relationship with Nathalie comfortably proper, finally costs him that same relationship.[30] At the end of the novel, his one approximation of any real involvement with another has ended, and he has "lost his place in the human community."[31]

The professor sustains one other large illusion through to the conclusion of the book. He continues to be most impressed by the supposed superior qualities of Miss Haldin. Even while she is telling him that her future course of action will be precisely as he "wished it," he "marvelled at" her "perfection of collected independence" (p. 373). He claims that her final words, "at last the anguish of hearts shall be extinguished in love," represent a deep "wisdom" and sees her leaving his life "wedded to an invincible belief in the advent of loving concord" (p. 377). But his evaluation of Natalia merely reflects her own view of herself, a view that her actions substantially compromise.

Nathalie regularly advocates "loving concord." When Razumov asks her if she believes that revenge is a duty, she eloquently and most emphatically responds: "Listen, Kirylo Sidorovitch. I believe that the future will be merciful to us all. Revolutionist and reactionary, victim and executioner, betrayer and betrayed, they shall all be pitied together when the light breaks on our black sky at last. Pitied and forgotten; for without that there can be no union and no love" (p. 353). Yet the conclusion of the novel demonstrates that Nathalie herself "is incapable ... of forgiving Razumov."[32] The proponent of pity, union, and love will not at all abide by her pronouncements when Razumov is revealed as the "reactionary," the "executioner," and the "betrayer."

Razumov looked behind a veil to see what the extent of Natalia's suffering might be and what that suffering would mean as an index to his own nature. Natalia, however, cannot return the favor. She does not see through the veil (appropriately, her own veil) in which he wrapped his final message to perceive that the written confession, attempting to explain the nature and cause of his duplicity, is also a plea for understanding and forgiveness. When he suffers the full consequences of his confessions, confessions prompted by his love for her, she does not visit him in the hospital and even smiles complacently as she observes that Tekla disapproves of her for this lack of sympathy. Her rhetoric of forgiveness rings false, for "she 'loves suffering mankind' but not a suffering man," a man who suffers, in the final analysis, mostly for her sake.[33]

"The truth shining in you," Razumov writes to Nathalie, "drew the truth out of me" (p. 361). Conrad ironically suggests that no truth shone in Nathalie. Razumov, because of his love, confesses to free himself from duplicity. He will no longer be deluded or deluding. Yet the love that prompts his confession is itself founded on illusion. Moreover, if he anticipated any understanding and forgiveness — and his last letter suggests that he does — then he is necessarily mistaken. Resembling the narrator in this respect, Razumov accepted Nathalie on her own terms and believed she was what she claimed to be. Only when it is too late to profit from such knowledge is he given the opportunity to discover he was wrong.

Conrad also demonstrates that Razumov continues to be the victim of other mistakes and misjudgments. For example, he terminates his confession to the revolutionaries by claiming he has rendered himself "free from falsehood, from remorse — independent of every single human being on this earth" (p. 368). Immediately thereafter Nikita puts out his eardrums. Instead of being independent of all, he is further isolated from all. His deafness, in fact, soon makes him most dependent on others. After the accident with the tramcar, he survives only because Tekla devotes herself to caring for him. She comes forward as "a relation" and becomes an obvious stand-in for the mother Razumov never had, partly because she has a vocation for mothering, partly because she sees him as a hero of the revolution, and partly because she also sees him as a reembodiment of her dead "poor Andrei." Razumov, who dreamed of fame, is left, at the end of the novel, totally dependent on poor Tekla and her illusions. He has been reduced to a helpless substitute child, a crippled ersatz hero, and a dying replacement for an originally pathetic lover.

Yet Jackson Heimer can still conclude a study of *Under Western Eyes* with the assertion that Razumov is finally fully redeemed. "By the novel's end love has helped him move from his almost Nietzschean aloofness, as it does Raskolnikov, into the world of men. He becomes *l'homme engagé* — the king wise in mind and heart."[34] One must insist that he becomes nothing of the sort. A deaf man slowly dying, tended by a substitute mother who sees him as a pseudo-lover and labors under the illusion that he is a revolutionary hero, Razumov has not elevated himself above the common level of man and in no way achieves the greatness he originally desired. His final condition is described by Sophia Antonovna who tells of where and how he lives. Confined to "a little two-roomed wooden house, in the suburb of some very small town, hiding within the high plank-fence of a yard overgrown with nettles," and "crippled, ill, getting weaker every day" (p. 379), he is hardly a man who has at last claimed some lofty position in life.

Furthermore, even Razumov's thoroughly marginal position is compromised by the novel's conclusion. Sophia Antonovna admits that he is occasionally visited. "Some of *us* always go to see him when passing through. He is intelligent. He has ideas. . . . He talks well, too" (p. 379). This information does not attest that Razumov is now safe at last in the bosom of the revolutionary party. The visits referred to might well be acts of conscience which derive from the more sensitive revolutionaries' recognizing that they are partly responsible for Razumov's final condition. As Sophia Antonovna notes, "he was the victim of an outrage" that "was not authorized" (p. 380). We can also recall that Razumov himself, in his last letter to Nathalie, insisted that she should not "be deceived"; despite his confession, he is "not converted" (p. 361). There is simply no evidence to prove that sometime later he does accept the revolutionaries' ideology to become a full member of their community.[35] In fact, Sophia Antonovna's phrasing ("Some of *us* always go to see him when passing through") implies that *others* of *us* do not. And how many of them would ever pass through that small town anyway? In brief, Conrad provides no basis for demonstrating that his protagonist has been incorporated into either the limited world of the revolutionaries or the vastly larger "world of men."

One must also insist that Heimer's comparison of Razumov and Raskolnikov is invalid. There is, admittedly, a definite similarity between the two novels, and Conrad no doubt wrote *Under Western Eyes* with a conscious awareness of what Dostoeyevsky had already done in *Crime and Punishment.*[36] But Razumov's final condition in no way resembled Raskolnikov's, and Conrad's conclusion does not parallel Dostoevsky's. As Baines observes, the two "confessions [Raskolnikov's and Razumov's] emphasize above all the difference between the two authors."[37] If anything, Conrad parodies the ending of the earlier novel. Raskolnikov, accepting a deserved punishment, is sent to Siberia. His eastward journey brings, finally, a recognition of the transcendent truth embodied in Sonia — who fully forgives the murder of her friend to love and accompany the murderer — and a consequent regeneration and rebirth. Razumov, after a grotesque punishment, one which he does not really deserve and one inflicted by a man far more guilty than he, is abandoned by the woman he loves and goes eastward to stagnation and impending death. His Sonia is Tekla, not the embodiment of any higher truth but a disillusioned idealist idealistically serving her most recent illusions.

As several critics have noted, *Under Western Eyes* is essentially concerned with the nature of ideas, with problems of how men think and fail to think.[38] Fleishman, for example, maintains that "the maturity of the novel lies in its focus upon the intellectual in the modern world."[39] Tanner claims that the novel portrays "the tragedy of 'a man with a mind.' "[40] Dostoevsky, too, was aware of this tragedy. In *Crime and Punishment* he dramatized the sterility inherent in calculated rationality. Raskolnikov, freeing himself from all external limitations to follow the promptings of his own reason, "acts out the terrifying consequences of being free."[41] But Dostoevsky envisions an escape from such burdensome freedom. He resolves the basic issue of this novel "by nudging Raskolnikov into God's camp."[42] A Christian who selflessly serves God and loves his fellow men escapes from the rationalist's error and illusion, the calculator's devisive concern for self.

Conrad provides no such solution. At the end of *Under Western Eyes,* Razumov, deaf and dying, is still mostly distinguished, as Sophia Antonovna observes, by his basic capabilities. "He is intelligent. He has ideas. . . . He talks well, too" (p. 379). These are the precise capabilities that distinguished him at the beginning of the novel. And the novel attests to how little they served him. His intelligence can finally only show him how disastrously he misapplied it in his past, how often he was wrong. Thus the novel, as Tanner maintains, "is the compelling account of a man forced into wide-awakeness, a man unwillingly made intimate with the nightmare that hovers forever just under the complacencies of civilized existence."[43] Dostoevsky suggested that one could awake from the nightmare, could discover an absolute solution to the problem of human limitations and could thus transcend the fallibility of reason. For Conrad, one awakens to the nightmare and by awakening more fully discovers the extent of human fallibility. There is, then, a cruel and tragic irony in the final vision of *Under Western Eyes.* It is the intelligent man who most fully perceives his own and humankind's stupidity. For this character there is no escape; not even ignorance can be bliss.

5

Limited Triumphs in *Victory*

Tony Tanner's summation of *Under Western Eyes* could also apply to *Victory,* for *Victory* too portrays a man "forced into wide-awakeness" and finally "made intimate with the nightmare" implicit in his life. But the two nightmares are not the same. Razumov's derives from his ambition, from his belief that he can rationally confront an irrational world. Since the supposed values of ambition and reason are more widely acknowledged than are the absurdities — even in its political manifestations — of life, Razumov's nightmare is common. It "hovers," for anyone, "just under the complacencies of civilized existence." Axel Heyst's nightmare is both different and differently located. It underlies the very scheme he designed to allow himself to pass "through life without suffering and almost without a single care in the world — invulnerable because elusive."[1] His particular nightmare is, in fact, one that befalls him largely because he was awake to the more general nightmare and attempted to elude it. "Determined to remain free from [the] absurdities of existence" (p. 202), he would not be another victim of what he termed "the Great Joke" (p. 198). Yet his efforts to circumvent that common fate finally make him victim of an even more cruelly ironic joke. He finds that thought, like action, is also a hook both barbed and baited.

For a number of critics, however, *Victory* derives largely from the immediately preceding popular *Chance.* Gary Geddes, for example, suggests we "misread" *Victory* unless we "see [it] as a continuing exploration of the aesthetic and philosophical concern given shape in *Chance.*"[2] J.I.M. Stewart more specifically maintains that these two books exhibit "an almost identical theme"; that *Victory,* paralleling *Chance,* also tells "the story of a distressed girl, rescued and carried into near solitude by a compassionate man, with a resulting period of strain and imperfect relationship which is only resolved — but by this time to a wholly tragic issue — by the irruption of villainy and violence."[3] Such an assessment emphasizes the romance elements in *Victory* — the lovers isolated on their tropical island; the intrusion of evil into what might have become a paradise of two. But Stewart's summary of the plot, accurate so far as it goes, does not hint at how the events in this novel regularly resonate with larger meanings. I would suggest that these larger meanings — centering on illusion, delusion, and the general human capability to be deceived, especially by and about oneself — serve to link *Victory* not with *Chance* but with the novel that came before that experiment in popularity, the darker and more pessimistic *Under Western Eyes.*[4]

To start with, it should be noted that the protagonists in *Under Western Eyes* and *Victory* are both prospective philosophers. Razumov is, at the beginning of *Under Western Eyes,* a student of philosophy. And even after he must terminate his career as a student, his association with philosophy continues. In Geneva, he broods and writes beneath the statue of Jean Jacques Rousseau; the setting for the climax of the novel is a house significantly located on the Boulevard de Philosophes. Heyst is even more dominated by philosophy. He is the son and the successor-disciple of a philosopher father. Indeed, Axel Heyst's whole existence is largely determined by his desire to live according to the principles implicit in his father's metaphysics.[5]

Even though the younger Heyst has largely inherited his philosophy, he is, nevertheless, a more convincing philosopher than is Razumov. The former is portrayed as a man who thinks, who is concerned with the ontological dimensions of existence, and who attempts to guide his own conduct according to a systematic assessment of the human condition. In short, Axel Heyst, like his father (roughly modeled on Schopenhauer), can be seen as a real philosopher whereas Razumov is only ostensibly one. The young Russian student was, after all, a prospective philosopher primarily because he believed he might make of that discipline a road to public prominence and perhaps a political career. He prepares for his chosen profession in order to gain a place in society and make his mark in the world. In this respect, he rather resembles numerous protagonists of more traditional *Bildungsromans* who, with essentially the same objectives, embrace such diverse occupations as politics or the priesthood, the army or the arts. Furthermore, it is not Razumov's philosophy which fails him but the basic plan that originally prompted him to study philosophy. His aborted career does not prove, then, the shortcomings of any particular philosophical system. Instead, it attests to the fallacies inherent in the optimism frequently implicit in the *Bildungsroman,* a comfortable assumption that the power of positive action should elevate almost any young man possessed of no particular social distinctions to fame and fortune, happiness and success.

"When novelists tell us that a character is a thinker," F.R. Leavis observes, "we have usually only their word for it."[6] Such is not the case with Axel Heyst. The entire novel bears out the narrator's statement that Heyst "had been used to think clearly and sometimes even profoundly, seeing life outside the flattering optical delusion of everlasting hope, of conventional self-deceptions, of an ever-expected happiness" (p. 82). Heyst has, of course, long seen through the "conventional self-deceptions" that so motivated Razumov and prompted his desperate desire to achieve some distinctive position. But it is Heyst's superior perceptiveness that, paradoxically, most significantly connects *Victory* and *Under Western Eyes.* Well aware of what Razumov only slowly and painfully learns, Heyst, in his private philosophy, begins at approximately the same point where the other ends. The young Russian student struggled to achieve honor and status; thwarted in that attempt he would at least demonstrate his capabilities for evil. In short, he is committed to purposeful action. The mature Swedish baron, however, explicitly denounces action as "the barbed hook, baited with the illusion of progress, to bring out of the lightless void the shoals of unnumbered generations" (p. 174). He decides, "austerely, from conviction," to drift aimlessly and sees such a program as his "defence against life" (p. 92).

By the end of the novel that defence has been thoroughly breached. Although he begins with an awareness that should protect him from such tragedies as the one that befell Razumov, this same awareness does not keep Heyst from suffering a different tragic fate. He had "often asked" himself, "with a momentary dread, in what way would life try to get hold of me?" (p. 202). In the fourth and final section of *Victory,* he discovers the answer. So once more it is appropriate to assess the ending of a specific work, for any satisfactory interpretation of Conrad's last major and "most controversial novel" must elucidate the causes and examine the implications of Axel Heyst's final act, his self-inflicted death by fire.[7]

By the end of part three of *Victory,* Heyst, who has twice transgressed against the teachings of his father and the supposed design of his own life — first by coming to Morrison's aid and then by rescuing Lena from the grotesquely overamorous advances of Schomberg — has also begun to discover that each "apostacy" might well involve more unfortunate consequences than he had first assumed. He had earlier "deemed himself guilty of Morrison's death" despite the fact that, as the narrator notes, "no one could possibly have foreseen the horrors of the cold, wet summer lying in wait for poor Morrison at home" (p. 65). But his "absurd feeling" of responsibility is soon magnified, for the first effect of the second apostacy is that he must confront more directly one result of the first. After he has carried Lena off to his island, he tells her of his previous fall from his conception of grace and concludes by finally naming the individual who encumbered him with undesired gratitude: "Truth, work, ambition, love itself, may be only counters in the lamentable or despicable game of life, but when one takes a hand one must play the game. No, the shade of Morrison needn't haunt me. What's the matter? I say, Lena, why are you staring like that? Do you feel ill?" (p. 203). To explain her reaction, Lena must recount the Schomberg fable of Heyst the spider and Morrison the fly. Heyst thereby discovers "how the business looked from outside" (p. 208). Despite his claims that the opinions of others cannot touch him, he is strangely "hurt" by the calumny. The "shade of Morrison," revived by vicious gossip, can continue to "haunt" him, as is later even more clearly demonstrated by the arrival of Mr. Jones and his company.

Furthermore, even as Heyst tells of the pathetically comic relationship that resulted from his rescue of Morrison, he expresses himself in terms that both foreshadow and partly precipitate subsequent misunderstandings between himself and Lena. More specifically, as "counters" in the lamentable game of life, "truth, work, ambition" can all ostensibly apply only to labor on behalf of Morrison's envisioned success of the Tropical Belt Coal Company and thereby register Heyst's reluctant participation in the joint venture. But "love" obviously cannot. It must, at least unconsciously, relate to Heyst and Lena. No wonder she is later determined to prove that her "love" is more than just another one of those "counters," even though the attempt brings death to them both. In fact, throughout the entire dialogue, Heyst is, as Bruce Johnson rightly notes, "insensitive to the extrapolations Lena continually and with every right makes."[8] From early comments about how, with Morrison, "boredom came later" (p. 199), and, "I only know that he who firms a tie is lost" (pp. 199-200), to later observations such as, "No, I've never killed a man or loved a woman — not even in my thoughts, not even in my dreams" (p. 212), the otherwise scrupulously courtesous and tactful Swedish baron callously overlooks how Lena must apply his statements to her own situation. And at the same time, because Lena does not adequately appreciate his unarticulated feelings and emotions, he also becomes angered to the point that, "for a moment," suddenly "he detested her" (p. 215).

Their relationship continues to be less than the perfect union of two sympathetic souls, as is further evidenced by Lena's request, soon after they have returned to the bungalow, that Heyst "should try to love" her (p. 221). This comment, like others before it, is interpreted as an attempt "to pick a very unnecessary quarrel." Then, confronting her continued silence, Heyst transforms his tentative charge into a confession of ignorance and admits, "I don't even understand what I have done or left undone to distress you like this" (p. 222). She need not be concerned, he reassures her, about any possible pitfalls that might lie before either one of them. "In our future, as in what people call the other life, there is nothing to be frightened of" (p. 222). And as to the scandal regarding Morrison: "Let us forget it. There's that in you, Lena, which can console me for worse things, for uglier passages. And if we forget, there are no voices here to remind us." Continuing in that same vein, he concludes: "Nothing can break in on us here" (p. 223), whereupon Wang, Heyst's native servant, intrudes to report, "Boat out there" (p. 224). Mr. Jones and his entourage have been spotted.

The consequences of having twice stooped to pet a "bad dog" world become more ominous as the novel progresses. Conrad also demonstrates how interrelated his protagonist's two slips are. Heyst has just found out that aiding Morrison led to "abominable calumny" (p. 218). That calumny, the rumor that the Swedish baron possesses certain cunningly acquired "plunder," provides Jones with a motive for visiting him, just as Heyst's rescue of Lena provides Schomberg with a motive for sending Jones. The arrival of the three intruders — an indirect consequence of both apostasies — also tests the direct result of the second one, the relationship that Heyst and Lena are attempting to establish. Furthermore, Jeffrey Berman points out that there are "symbolic and psychological connections. . . between the arrival of the unholy trio and the rapidly deteriorating relationship of Heyst and Lena."[9] In effect, the intruders objectify the very divisions that their presence also magnifies.

Heyst and Lena, somewhat at cross purposes before their threatening guests arrive, are even more so afterwards. Thus the very next night when Lena "woke up from a painful dream of separation brought about in a way she could not understand" (p. 250), she finds Heyst searching for his missing revolver and reads into his questions an accusation that he did not intend. As Robert Haugh observes, the fact that she thinks he "suspects her of theft" shows that "they are still strangers to one another."[10] And strangers they remain, for they are not drawn together by the trial that they both face. Instead, as Jones and Ricardo attempt to validate their view of Heyst's first success — the fleecing of Morrison supposedly justifies the fleecing of Heyst — the two outlaws only prove the extent of their reluctant host's second failure. The test that was supposed to reveal one pattern of Heyst's duplicity exposes another.

The testing begins at once with Ricardo's aborted assault on Lena, an attack that also doubly demonstrates the general incapability of Mr. Jones's faithful secretary. Most obviously, he fails to achieve his immediate objective of raping the girl even though the attack is described with an authorial insistence on the perpetrator's seemingly irresistable savagery. When Ricardo sees Lena, "defenceless — and tempting," behind a curtain, doing her hair, "the instinct for the feral spring could not longer be denied. Ravish or kill — it was all one to him, as long as by the act he liberated the suffering soul of savagery repressed for so long" (p. 288). He gives "a quick glance over his shoulder, which hunters of big game tell us no lion or tiger omits to give before charging home," and then he himself charges, "head down, straight at the curtain" (pp. 288-89). No wonder one critic sees the secretary at this point "metamorphosed into a beast of the jungle."[11] But no such transformation takes place. Ricardo, who has hitherto been presented as the very personification of the ferociously feline, immediately proves to be more tabby than tiger, and "Lena subdues him with almost childish ease."[12] It should also be remembered that Lena's assailant earlier boasted to Schomberg of his way with women: "Take 'em by the throat or chuck 'em under the chin is all one to me

— almost" (p. 166). How appropriate that she, with a "murderous clutch on Ricardo's windpipe" (p. 292), chokes him into submission and even a grudging admiration of *her* prowess.

The inept attack is also suggestive in a second sense. Ricardo's fertile imagination had earlier evoked an irresistible image of "eminently portable" treasure, and he had then gone on to envision where the, for him, indubitably real "canvas bags" or "steel cash-boxes" might have been hidden: "The darkness of the forest at night, and in it the gleam of a lantern, by which a figure is digging at the foot of a tree-trunk. As likely as not, another figure holding that lantern — ha, feminine! The girl!" (p. 274). On the basis of this deduction, the secretary proceeds to plot. Lena must be persuaded to betray her baron, which should not be too difficult. "She couldn't be much. He knew that sort" (p. 282). Nevertheless, "he felt" it "was *very necessary*" to "form some opinion about" the girl and thereby determine what approach to employ "before venturing on some steps to get in touch with her behind that Swedish baron's back" (p. 282, emphasis added). Prowling through Heyst's bungalow, he is seeking a chance to appraise his prospective co-conspirator, when he discovers her behind the "unforeseen veil." In light of these considerations, Ricardo's immediate "charge," proves, as much as does the subsequent botched assault, his general incompetence. He can execute neither an impulsive transgression nor a planned one. Furthermore, the impulse certainly runs counter to the plan. He cannot, by raping the girl, come to know her in any useful fashion and neither will he, with that act, encourage her to abandon Heyst and betray the hiding place of the hypothetical treasure. Yet Ricardo, quite unaware of all probable consequences, including the substantial possibility of distinctly displeasing his patron, plunges through the symbolically suggestive "veil" to discover still another error. He has misestimated the capabilities of the "defenceless" girl.

Ricardo continues on the same course of error. Just as he was certain he could comprehend Lena before he had so much as seen her, he is, after the fiasco of the attempted rape, even more positive that his suddenly revised estimation represents a full assessment of her character. He need not even apologize for the attack. She will "know how it is," just as he "can see, now," that rape "wasn't the way" to win her favor (p. 294). Soon he is even assuming that they are practically soulmates: "Born alike, bred alike," and so "made to understand each other" (p. 297). With such mutual understanding ostensibly established, Ricardo concludes that his original plan can now be put into effect. He turns his attention to the treasure; questions Lena; and from her gestures and half answers and calculated duplicity, decides that she does not yet know where Heyst has hidden "the swag" but that her baron "could be brought to trust" her (p. 297). He is inviting her to "stand in with us" (p. 279) and receive her "share — of the plunder" (p. 300), even as she sees in him "the embodied evil of the world" (p. 298). In short, they each radically misjudge the other. Ricardo, as previously noted, is hardly the personification of savagery that he pretends to be. Lena is appalled at the idea of some partnership with thieves. All they can offer her is the opportunity to prove her love for Heyst.

While Ricardo anticipates employing Lena to achieve one of his prime objectives, she also sees that he might serve one of hers. Earlier, during her long exchange with Heyst just before the arrival of the invaders, she had "felt in her innermost depths an irresistible desire to give herself up to him more completely, by some act of absolute sacrifice" (p. 201). She might thereby refute his courteous contemning of love. Now Ricardo provides her with the opportunity to do so. Sensing the drift of his comments, she encourages him to run on. He soon obligingly suggests how she might give a more definite shape to her dream when he tells her of the knife he carries strapped to his leg. A dream, however, is not a definite program. As the narrator notes, Lena "had no plan" (p. 308). Nevertheless, when Heyst, entering immediately after Ricardo's hasty departure, lifts the emotionally depleted girl to carry her into the bedroom, "a thrill went through her at the sudden thought that it was she who would have to protect him" (p. 309).

Something of her reaction shows. Heyst, noting that Lena is not her usual self, briefly wonders about the "new mystery" before deciding that "there is some very simple explanation, no doubt" (p. 309). In other words, he comprehends Lena no better than did Ricardo, which is not surprising, for Heyst, at this point, is really preoccupied with other mysteries. As he soon tells Lena, he has just concluded a perturbing interview with Mr. Jones and has heard the "merry skeleton" advance strange claims of satanic capability. For example, the other maintained that, "coming and going up and down the earth," he was "no blacker" and "neither more nor less" determined than the first "gentleman" who followed that same course (pp. 317-18). Heyst, however, found such hyperbole particularly problematic because Jones also claimed that his inflated account of himself equally applied to the Swedish baron. They had, he insisted, "much more in common" than the recipient of that observation would admit, for Jones was simply more honest in pursuing his objectives.

Heyst insists Jones's words were only "a jeer," but does so too vehemently — striking the table as he speaks — to be convincing. He apparently senses that there is more to the other's statements than the intention to offend. Indeed, some similarities between the two men are obvious. Both are gentlemen; both have renounced the conventional existence of the well-born and well-bred; both have found companions from a lower social level. There are still other connections too. Heyst, even as the three invaders were rowing to his wharf, had momentarily "abandoned himself to the half-belief that something of his father dwelt yet on earth — a ghostly voice" (p. 219). And soon he finds himself in frequent conversation with one regularly described as a specter or a skeleton. This double hint (the timing of Jones's arrival as well as that gentleman's ghostly nature) suggests that Mr. Jones is a perverse reembodiment of the senior Heyst and his pessimistic philosophy of negation.[13] Heyst's father, in his last book, "claimed for mankind that right to absolute moral and intellectual liberty of which he no longer believed them worthy" (p. 91). Worthy or not, Jones claims for himself the same liberty, as indicated by his "indifferent" observation to Schomberg "that he depended on himself, as if the world were still one great, wild jungle without law" (p. 113). In short, Jones abandons all moral scruples and human considerations — factors which have no place in the abstract theories of either Heyst but which neither, especially the son, could completely ignore. Jones thereby becomes a possible reembodiment of Heyst's father and thus — since the son is his father's avatar too — a double for the son. As Jeffrey Meyers points out, Jones also insinuates that Heyst is "trying to repress and deny" his homosexuality, whereas he, Jones, is flamboyantly the real thing, and that posited partial parallel calls into question the obviously problematic matter of his host's sexuality.[14] No wonder the implied relationship between the two men so troubles Heyst.

However, as John Palmer rightly observes, "the identity between Heyst and Jones is not exact; rather, they are inverted images of one another."[15] Nevertheless, a connection still exists, and Heyst apparently recognizes at least its partial validity. At a time when he has already concluded that his two departures from his private philosophy represent personal failures and has come to see, painfully, how much the world misconstrued one of these actions, he is presented with still another obstacle to effective action. In moving, openly and decisively, against Jones, would he, as Jones suggests, really be acting like Jones?[16] Or, differently phrased, does his father's philosophy necessarily imply that the supposed morality of any "moral" action represents merely a construct of an imaginative will? For Heyst, the answer seems obvious. Because he suspects that "the use of reason is to justify the obscure desires that move our conduct, impulses, passions, prejudices and follies, and also our fears" (p. 83), he cannot rationally justify any action that might be prompted by his animosity towards Jones. Too honest to pretend what he cannot believe, he becomes more and more metaphysically disarmed.

That mental process has an obvious objective correlative, for a physical disarming occurs concomitant with the emotional one. First, the revolver is stolen. Soon afterwards, Wang removes himself, along with the purloined weapon, from the future field of battle, leaving Heyst to face his antagonists alone. Wang, withdrawing, also insists that Heyst and Lena cannot avail themselves of the possible refuge that the Alfura village might provide. But there is still another purpose served by this servant's armed retreat. Heyst feels called upon to warn Jones of the new state of affairs. Then, when his warning elicits only disbelief and the insistent suggestion that Jones's servant, Pedro, shall now cook for them all, the host must hide both his dismay and his desire to throttle his three guests. Like Lena earlier, Heyst is here forced into duplicity but, in contrast to the girl, he has no dream, no vestige of a plan. He recognizes that he has "refined everything away by this time — anger, indignation, scorn itself" (p. 329); yet he cannot feel the aloof indifference to any possible danger that should be the product of that process and the appropriate response to Jones's ominous innuendoes. As Heyst — again speaking rather tactlessly — laments to Lena: "And only three months ago I would not have cared. I would have defied their scoundrelism as much as I have scorned all the other intrusions of life. But now I have you! You stole into my life, and — "(p. 324). Prompted by such comments, Lena must continue to dream of somehow proving the value of her love.

She soon attempts to put her dream into action. After she and Heyst have returned from their futile attempt to find some safety with Wang, Ricardo arrives bringing an invitation from Mr. Jones requesting a private conference with Heyst. Lena gestures that he should accept. In his absence, she might find some way to save him. And Heyst, at that point, welcomes any hint. "In his state of doubt and disdain and almost of despair . . . he would let even a delusive appearance guide him through a darkness so dense that it made for indifference" (p. 365). He goes to call on Mr. Jones. "Her nod, imaginary or not imaginary, advice or illusion, had tipped the scale" (p. 366). The wording is not propitious, and neither is the phrasing with which the omniscient narrator describes Lena's reaction to Heyst's uncertain acquiescence. "In a *blinding,* hot glow of passionate purpose," she has resolved the "bitter riddle" of "her own existence" (p. 367, emphasis added). The hint implicit in that quotation is soon repeated. "She passed by Heyst as if she had indeed been *blinded* by some secret, lurid, and consuming glare into which she was about to enter" (p. 368, emphasis added). Blindness and delusion do seem to characterize the two actors in this scene.

They become no more perspicacious as the action in *Victory* rapidly winds to its conclusion. In fact, Conrad shows that both Heyst and Lena unwittingly retreat more and more into their own world of dream or delusion. Each thereby misleads and misestimates the other. For example, as Heyst, departing for his final encounter with Mr. Jones, leaves Lena, he significantly whispers only to himself her name. Not trusting himself to speak aloud, "not trusting himself — no, not even to the extent of a tender word" (p. 373), he, while lifting a curtain, silently looks back into the room. Here we have an odd conjunction — lifting a veil in order to go forth yet reluctantly looking back. The curtain is between Axel Heyst and the world. He is leaving his bungalow, a retreat dominated by his father's books and portrait (a correlative to his father-dominated life) and going forth to meet Mr. Jones — the reincarnated ghost of his father, his own perverted double, a personification of death and the Devil, the world paying

Heyst a visit, as well as "a sort of fate — the retribution that waits its time" (p. 379). He is, indeed, about to confront an antagonist that might well engage all his attention. But Heyst, although he is lifting a physical curtain, is not yet ready to penetrate through any metaphoric one. Leaving, looking back, he sees Lena "*plainly*, all black, down on her knees, . . . in the desolation of a mourning sinner" (p. 373, emphasis added). At that sight, the "suspicion that there were everywhere more things than he could understand crossed Heyst's mind," and he left perplexed, "full of disquiet" (p. 373). His disquieting suspicion is clearly well-founded. Heyst does not see Lena plainly, and neither does he perceive with any clarity his own feelings or situation. But the sentence resonates with larger meaning. The more one ponders the events of this novel, the more one suspects that "there is everywhere more than is understood."

To start with, Lena is supposedly wearing black merely because such dress is part of Heyst's final ineffectual attempt to cope with their visitors. She will hide in the forest watching for confused candle signals — if "you see three candles out of four blown out and one relighted," or, "wait until three candles are lighted and then two put out" (p. 372) — both of which will convey the same message that she is to return to him. While she is thus occupied, Heyst, with no real plan of action, no weapon, and no will to use it if one were provided, will try to dispose of Mr. Jones, Ricardo, and Pedro. The whole nebulous scheme demonstrates how inadequately Heyst is coping with his predicament — a fact which should be obvious to any thinking man. As Leo Gurko notes, the suggested candle signals themselves evince "a monumental ineptness."[17] But there is also much in the scene that Heyst could not be expected to perceive. Considering Lena's previous protestations of faithfulness and devotion — "I will do anything you like" (p. 308) — he cannot expect that she will disobey his explicit directive. He has even less reason to suspect that she too is planning to confront a double and has planned more definitely than he. Appropriately arranged in a black dress and with a dark veil, she is ready for a perverted marriage. She will surrender herself completely — sexually, if necessary — to Ricardo and will thus, theoretically, achieve her at last fully evolved dream. She will sacrifice herself so that Heyst might be saved, be saved by her.

Lena too, in a sense, is occupied with veils. Behind one veil, she is trying to remove another, for she recognizes that Heyst's playful courtesy, his noncommittal smile, and his aloofness from life are all part of a curtain that, hanging between him and her, prevents her from having any real role in his life. She has heard him tell, at length, of Morrison. Afraid of being another reluctantly tolerated victim of Heyst's charity and a recipient of "that form of contempt which is called pity" (p. 174), she wants to do such a great deed that she will win a place forever in "the sanctuary of his inner-most heart" (p. 407). She has decided she must "disarm murder itself" (p. 397), and in this enterprise she is to a degree successful. That is her victory. But it is an ambiguous and uncertain victory and becomes more so the more one examines it. In fact, the tragedy of errors with which the work ends mostly derives from Lena's dream and her partial success at achieving it.

"In the fourth part of *Victory,*" Frederick Karl rightly observes, Lena more and more occupies "the center of the novel."[18] But his subsequent assertion that "everyone except her in one way or another is being deluded" rather overstates the case, for Lena is no exception to a general rule. As the final scenes unfold, Ricardo is mistaken about Lena; Heyst and Mr. Jones are both mistaken about Lena; and Lena too is mistaken about herself and what she can do. She has, for instance, only half-comprehended Heyst's character and quite misjudges what both his immediate reaction and his final response to her self-sacrifice might be. She certainly did not plan to cause his suicide. In short, from the beginning (the various attempts to define Heyst) until the very end, much of the action in the novel turns on mistakes and misunderstandings. As Geddes rightly observes of Heyst and Lena: "Each is trying to write the novel of the other."[19] And all the other major characters are diligently composing their own fictions too.

At first, however, it seems as if some basic errors might be resolved and their possible consequences forestalled. During Heyst's and Jones's final interview, the truth about Schomberg's jealous lying emerges. The rabidly misogynistic Mr. Jones discovers that there is a woman on the island. That first discovery immediately prompts a second one. Ricardo, just assessed as one "absolutely identified with all my ideas, wishes, and even whims" (p. 379), obviously does not share his patron's antipathy towards women. Doubly deceived, the "governor," enraged, determines to be avenged. Yet this determination does not prove that Jones is what Heyst previously decided he must be, "an absolutely hard and pitiless scoundrel" (p. 382). Heyst himself revises that too-flattering estimation as he finds out how uninformed Jones is about the state of his prospective victim's affairs. The other's claim that he and Martin were "adequate bandits" is soon countered by Heyst's more accurate comment "that there were never in the world two more deluded bandits — never!" (p. 384). "What sort of comedy is this?" Heyst asks, while Jones's "shocked incredulity — something like frightened disgust" (p. 386) — and ludicrously expressed rage carry that comedy even further towards the absurd: "And he [Ricardo] shaved — shaved under my very nose. I'll shoot him!" (p. 387).

The forces of evil are split, yet this new situation offers no advantage to Heyst. As Jones gives way to his anger, indulging in the pathetically perverse fulminations of a disappointed lover and even "executing a dance of rage in the middle of the floor" (p. 389), Heyst recognizes that he could then dispose of this antagonist, "but he did not move" to do so (p. 387). Unmanned, he still cannot act decisively. "Like a prisoner captured by the evil power of a masquerading skeleton" (p. 390), he follows Mr. Jones back to his bungalow believing they will discover Ricardo "rifling [his] desk" (p. 382) or in some other way "ransacking [his] house" (p. 389). Again he is mistaken. The two come on a scene that is, for Jones, a "disgusting spectacle" (p. 391); for Heyst, even worse. The man who, moments before, thought "his very will" was "dead of weariness" (p. 390) experiences "a doubt of a new kind, formless, hideous" (p. 391), and is decimated by a sight that "seemed to sear his very brain" (p. 392). In the "intolerable brilliance" (p. 392) of eight burning candles, he sees Lena sitting "as if enthroned. . . her head dreamily inclined on her breast," and "seemingly without strength, yet without fear, tenderly stooping" (p. 391). We soon find to what she is stooping. "I'll be anything you like," she had said to Ricardo (p. 400). But that representative of unrestrained animal appetite suffers from what one critic of Conrad, who is also a practicing psychiatrist, describes as a "most blatantly erotic example of foot-fetishism."[20] The sob-like "gasping words" and "little noises . . . of grief and distress" (p. 401) that Ricardo utters as he presses kiss after kiss onto Lena's instep almost anticipate the comic pornography of a more contemporary writer such as Terry Southern.

Again, however, there is much more to a scene than meets the eye. Ricardo, as he indulges in his particular sexual proclivities, also worships the Virgin of his choice, who, in keeping with *Victory*'s pervasive parody of Biblical themes, clearly is not one.[21] Lena is surrendering to Ricardo, yet the surrender is incomplete, partly because he is a fetishist and partly because she had already substantially unmanned him when she rather easily thwarted the attempted rape. But now she is even more successful in emasculating, at least figuratively, this former would-be ravisher. She persuades him to give up his knife, a weapon that he always wears strapped to his leg and that, although rarely produced, continually reassures him of his potency.[22]

Lena's whole plan can be interpreted in terms of Freudian and phallic symbolism. She is both literally and figuratively serving Heyst. The man she loves is weaponless, so she will provide him with one. But the man she loves is also unmanned. His pistol has disappeared. When he contemplates alternate weapons he considers such phallic implements as the crowbar or a knife, yet he does no more than consider. He realizes that even if he did have a weapon, he could not use it. Indeed, Heyst himself, with his earlier quoted observation that he has never killed or loved, suggests something of his metaphysical impotence. His problem, therefore, is not simply the skepticism that is his legacy from a too-much-dominating father. He is a common figure in twentieth-century literature, a sexually marred man whose incapacity mirrors the sterility of the world in which he lives (a forerunner, for example, of Jake Barnes). Surrounded by the dregs of Morrison's dream of action, Heyst is even the maimed ruler of an empty land and thus also anticipates T.S. Eliot's "The Waste Land." Lena at least partly perceives his predicament. At one point she thinks that "she would have liked to lock him up by some stratagem" while she disposed of the invaders, for "he seemed to her too good for such contacts, and *not sufficiently equipped*" (p. 317, emphasis added). Later she evolves a different strategy. If she can capture the sexual potency of Ricardo and pass it on to Heyst, might not the latter be cured? How terribly ironic that Ricardo, a heterosexual fetishist with apparent homosexual leanings, is also sexually marred.

Heyst, however, has no way of knowing what Lena might intend. Standing beside Mr. Jones, he views the other couple very much as Mr. Jones views them. He believes that he sees the girl surrendering to Ricardo and seemingly enjoying the surrender. The scene fills him with a "formless, hideous" doubt that makes "the earth, the sky itself" tremble and shake (pp. 391-92). He asks if he has any reason to continue living, if perhaps he is not already dead. Consequently, although Lena intended to draw Heyst back to life, the immediate result of her sacrifice is the exact opposite. By pushing him into a "spectral fellowship" (p. 393) with the "skeleton out of a grave" (p. 390), she succeeds only in further "unmanning" the man she dreamed she could save.

Conrad also here emphasizes the logical inconsistency of Lena's final actions. To win the love of one man, she will sacrifice herself to another. To render Heyst capable, she will do for him what he could not do for himself and exults in her ability to do so. There is even a hint that she might really prefer Heyst unmanned. When she gives him the knife she also instructs him not to use it. Perhaps the woman who, in Murray Krieger's phrasing, "glories in Heyst's incapacities because of what they leave only her to do," does not want to see him suddenly capable.[23] Moreover, as Sharon Kaehele and Howard German point out, Lena, towards the end of the novel, increasingly becomes Ricardo's double. The two followers both redirect their loyalties. Ricardo abandons Mr. Jones for a dream of Lena's love, while Lena, more insidiously, abandons Heyst for a dream of Heyst's love.[24] The latter "betrayal" is more insidious because it is almost impossible to recognize as an abandonment. Mr. Jones, in contrast to Heyst, readily notices the manner in which he has been deceived and at once sees how to respond to Ricardo's defection.

Further associating Lena with Ricardo, to whom life was a "game of grab," and with Mr. Jones too, a professional gambler, is the fact that, whatever else she is doing, Lena is gambling. Moreover, she gambles in a game in which she knows neither the rules nor the stakes. What does she risk in her encounter with Ricardo? What might she win in return? There is, indeed, little that she can gain, when one considers that a quick trip to "the armoury" (p. 402), "loaded to the very brim with weapons," can supply Ricardo with implements more deadly than his knife.[25] But Lena never fully considers such questions. As the narrator explicitly notes: "She reckoned upon nothing definite; she had calculated nothing." Instead, "she saw only her purpose of capturing death — savage, sudden, irresponsible death, prowling round the man who possessed her" (p. 394). Conrad, however, clearly demonstrates that the reasons for which she thinks she gambles are fallacious.

Contrary to what Seymour Gross claims, Lena certainly does not reenact the Biblical victory of "crushing the serpent's head."[26] In fact, the very passage Gross quotes to prove her triumph compromises his interpretation. "The viper's head" was "*all but* lying under her heel" (p. 399, emphasis added). Ricardo was not yet underfoot but "crept closer and closer to the chair in which she sat." He arrives, not to be crushed, but to engage in the parodic foot-kissing previously described. We are also told that Lena's attention was totally centered on the problem of "how to keep possession of that weapon which had *seemed* to have drawn into itself every danger and menace on the deathridden earth" (p. 399, emphasis again added). The immediately subsequent deaths of Lena herself, Pedro, Ricardo, Jones, and Heyst show, however, that there are more roads to premature mortality than by way of one particular knife.

Nothing is won when Ricardo surrenders his knife. Lena cannot use it and neither can Heyst. In fact, the entire gambit with Ricardo is superfluous. By merely revealing her presence, Lena could have disposed of Mr. Jones and his entourage. All she really wins is death, which comes soon after she receives the bullet intended for Ricardo. And even in dying, she miscounts her winnings. She sees herself lifted up into Heyst's "innermost heart — for ever!" (p. 407). Yet that heart remains as humanly uninhabitable as it previously was. "His fastidious soul" has not changed; "even at that moment" it "kept the true cry of love from his lips in its infernal mistrust of all life" (p. 406). She does not even save Heyst. He obviously comprehends his own failure much more clearly than he understands her sacrifice. But whatever he comes to see, it is not the optimistic affirmation that an out-of-context reading of his final words can imply. As Kingsley Widmer indisputably observes, a "flaming suicide is not 'trust in life.' "[27] Heyst remains allied with Mr. Jones, and both go to self-inflicted deaths.

Heyst's final message could, in fact, mean just what it says: "Woe to the man whose heart has not learned while young to hope, to love — and to put its trust in life" (p. 410).[28] The habits of hoping, loving, trusting, if acquired early enough, might blind one to the fact that hope, love, and trust are all ultimately as empty as Heyst's father said they were; that life, in the last analysis, is what it was for even Lena, "this lonely place" (p. 406) from which she wished to be carried. The great mistake, then, is not lowering a veil but lifting it. Nothing is sure. Lena's dream of love brings tragedy as much as does Heyst's fastidious aloofness. But the real tragedy is to see what both Heysts finally saw, to gaze on "the horror, the horror" of what men, particularly Western thinking men, can do.

That horror, for Conrad, can no longer be mitigated by thought, by evaluation and dawning self-awareness. In *Heart of Darkness,* Kurtz could still triumph over the nightmare in which he had played a leading role and did so by voicing his final judgment of his own life. Heyst and Jones, however, both make, with their suicides, more devastating self-condemnations, yet nothing is thereby redeemed. The two suicides are, if anything, a final parody of Christian myth. The death by water is soon followed by a death by fire. But no saving few survive the first minor apocalypse and the second one ushers in no new millennium.

Davidson, ending his account of the final events on Samburan Island, observes: "And then, your Excellencey, I went away. There was nothing to be done there." The key word, repeated, concludes the novel: "Davidson, thoughtful, seemed to weigh the matter in his mind, and then murmured with placid sadness: 'Nothing!' " (p. 412). As a recent critic has observed: "The novel ends with death regnant in Heyst's clearing on Samburan, while the forms of civilization are upheld only by the most impercipient of persons, Davidson, who can live placidly with 'Nothing' since the word has been domesticated by inclusion in the dreary context of an official report, where it offers no obtrusive metaphysical threat." William Bonney continues: "If once again the 'Son of David' (see, e.g., Matthew 1:1, 9:27, 15:22) redeems a world, he accomplishes the task only partially and in helpless ignorance, his very name serving only to confirm bleak ironic discrepancies that are for Conrad ontologically definitive."[29]

Yet something more can still be made of that concluding "Nothing!" Ian Watt uses the term "delayed decoding" to describe one of Conrad's basic "devices" for "giving direct narrative expression to the way in which the consciousness elicits meaning from expression."[30] The "sense impression" is provided first: its "meaning" or explanation is specified later; the reader is required to participate directly in the process of making rational sense out of perturbing impression. And the ending of *Victory*, I would finally suggest, provides the most extreme example of this technique in action. For Davidson, there is "nothing" to be done; this "nothing," however, remains to be decoded. The task is doubly difficult. The subsequently provided explanation comes only in the silence that sounds beyond the text's concluding word. It is, after all, "nothing" that we are required to comprehend more fully, but after that "nothing" what more can Conrad say to expand upon it or to delineate its limits? No wonder *Victory* was his last major work and he had to retreat, in the later books, from the full confrontation with life's flaws and futilities that we see in his five great novels.

Notes

Introduction

1. J. Hillis Miller, "The Problematic of Ending in Narrative," *Nineteenth-Century Fiction* 33 (1978), 4.

2. Marianna Torgovnick, *Closure in the Novel* (Princeton: Princeton University Press, 1981), p. 6.

3. Torgovnick, pp. 207-8.

4. Miller, p. 6.

5. Miller, p. 7.

6. David Daiches, *The Novel and the Modern World* (Chicago: University of Chicago Press, 1939), p. 2.

7. Alan Friedman, *The Turn of the Novel: The Transition to Modern Fiction* (New York: Oxford University Press, 1966), p. 15.

8. Friedman, pp. 21-22.

9. Friedman, p. 16.

10. Torgovnick observes that "the Modernist bias of critics like Friedman has virtually destroyed the usefulness of the term 'open' and 'closed' to describe endings, by making 'open' a term of approbation, and 'closed' a term linked with unadventurous and narrow didacticism" (pp. 9-10).

11. David H. Richter, *Fable's End: Completeness and Closure in Rhetorical Fiction* (Chicago: University of Chicago Press, 1974), p. 3.

12. Richter, p. 4.

13. Quoted from Stendahl's description of the novel in *The Red and the Black,* which is reprinted in *The Theory of the Novel,* ed. by Philip Stevick (New York: Free Press, 1967), p. 389.

14. Frank Kermode, *The Sense of an Ending: Studies in the Theory of Fiction* (New York: Oxford University Press, 1967), p. 140.

15. Kermode, p. 140.

16. Henry James, "Preface" to *Roderick Hudson* (1875; rpt. Harmondsworth: Penguin, 1969), p. 11.

17. E.M. Forster, *Aspects of the Novel* (New York: Harcourt, Brace, 1927), p. 143.

18. Richard Brautigan, *A Confederate General From Big Sur* (1964; rpt. New York: Grove 1970), p. 160.

19. Conrad's endings are also no less open (insofar as that elastic term can be pinned down) than any of the other experimental fictions just discussed, which should refute Friedman's claim that these same endings bring us only "to the threshold of the radical vision of conscience that shapes the flux of experience in the twentieth-century novel" (p. 105).

20. It might be noted that J. Hillis Miller, who most insists that the ending cannot be delineated from the rest of the text, also implicitly argues, in "Ariadne's Thread: Repetition and the Narrative Line," *Critical Inquiry* 3 (1976), 69, that it must: "The end of the story is the retrospective revelation of the law of the whole. That law is an underlying 'truth' which ties all together in an inevitable sequence revealing a hitherto hidden figure in the carpet."

Chapter 1

1. Suresh Raval, "Narrative and Authority in *Lord Jim:* Conrad's Art of Failure," *ELH* 48 (1981), 387. Much the same point has also been made by J. Hillis Miller who, in *Fiction and Repetition: Seven English Novels* (Cambridge, Mass.: Harvard University Press, 1982), p. 30, observes: "Certainly the final paragraphs of the novel show Marlow by no means 'satisfied.' The ending is a tissue of unanswered questions in which Marlow affirms once more not that Jim is a hero or that Jim is a coward, but that he remains an indecipherable mystery."

2. Jacques Berthoud, *Joseph Conrad: The Major Phase* (Cambridge, Eng.: Cambridge University Press, 1978), p. 66.

3. Miller, however, maintains that "when *Lord Jim* is approached from the perspective of its narrative structure and its design of recurrent images it reveals itself to be not less but more problematic, more inscrutable" (p. 31). Perhaps, but at least the nature of the problems can be partially clarified.

4. Robert F. Haugh, "The Structure of *Lord Jim,*" *College English* 13 (1951), 141.

5. Jocelyn Baines, *Joseph Conrad: A Critical Biography* (London: Weidenfeld and Nicolson, 1960), p. 251.

6. Elliott B. Gose, Jr., "Pure Exercise of Imagination: Archetypal Symbolism in *Lord Jim,*" *PMLA* 79 (1964), 147.

7. Ted E. Boyle, *Symbol and Meaning in the Fiction of Joseph Conrad* (The Hague: Mouton, 1965), p. 80.

8. Ian P. Watt, "The Ending of *Lord Jim,*" *Conradiana* 11 (1979), p. 19.

9. Paul S. Bruss, "Lord Jim and the Metaphor of Awakening," *Studies in the Twentieth Century,* No. 14 (1974), 70. Richard C. Stevenson, in "Stein's Prescription of 'How to Be' and the Problem of Assessing Lord Jim's Career," *Conradiana,* 7 (1975), also assesses how Jim's death has been evaluated. As he points out, some critics have postulated "romantic posturing and resounding failure" while others see only "resounding triumph" (p. 241). Stevenson attempts to resolve that dichotomy and does note some of the dubious aspects of Jim's last actions. But I would suggest that, in his conclusion, Stevenson falls

off the balance he is trying to strike: "Jim's final action, in its submission to the destructive element that he himself has created, is an act of atonement for his entire career" (p. 242). We have here the same old Jim redeemed again. And even apparent postulations of "posturing and . . . failure" are not always as critical as they might seem. Thus Thomas Moser, in *Joseph Conrad: Achievement and Decline* (Cambridge, Mass.: Harvard University Press, 1957), p. 35, observes that Jim's "quest for death" at the end of the novel indicates "an unconscious desire for self-destruction" which the author sees as a "fault." But it is a fault, Moser argues, that Conrad must "admire": "After all, it is Jim's 'intensity' that makes Marlow admit that Jim is 'none the less true.' " So here too we have Jim partially redeemed, redeemed now by the very "vigor" with which he courted his defeat. For more consistent recent condemnations of Jim's end, see H.M. Daleski, *Joseph Conrad: The Way of Dispossession* (New York: Holmes and Meier, 1976), pp. 99-103; and Paul Bruss, *Conrad's Early Sea Fiction: The Novelist as Navigator* (Lewisburg: Bucknell University Press, 1979), pp. 93-99.

10. From Commodore Sir Ivan Thompson's introduction to the little Collins Classics edition of *Lord Jim* and quoted by G.S. Fraser, "Lord Jim: The Romance of Irony," *Critical Quarterly* 8 (1966), 233.

11. *Lord Jim,* Canterbury Edition, Vol. 21 (New York: Doubleday and Page, 1924), p. 5. Subsequent references to this edition will be made parenthetically in the text.

12. Miller, p. 29.

13. Edward W. Said, *The World, The Text, and the Critic* (Cambridge, Mass.: Harvard University Press, 1983), p. 96.

14. Ann M. Gossman and George W. Whiting, "The Essential Jim," *Nineteenth-Century Fiction* 16 (1961), 77.

15. J.E. Tanner, "The Chronology and the Enigmatic End of *Lord Jim,*" *Nineteenth-Century Fiction* 21 (1967), 370.

16. Tanner, p. 371.

17. Raymond Gates Malbone, " 'How to Be': Marlow's Quest in *Lord Jim,*" *Twentieth Century Literature* 10 (1964-65), 175.

18. Brown, however, is by no means totally successful. When he stole the schooner, he did not take "the time to trans-ship enough provisions" (p. 356), and this first oversight foreshadows a second more serious one. The hunger for revenge that drove Brown to wreak havoc on Dain Waris and the other Bugis guarding the river also deprived him of the provisions that Jim had said he would send down the river. The result is that Brown's men die of starvation. Thus, if Brown is different from Jim in being initially more capable, he is also similar in that he demands to deal with the world on his own terms, which spells disaster as much for him as it did for Jim.

19. Marlow's account, in his letter, of how he first encountered the grieving Jewel imagistically implies her final condition. When he first sees her, she is mirrored by a "waxed floor" that seemed "a sheet of frozen water" (p. 347), while overhead the "crystals of a great chandelier clicked . . . like glittering icicles"; Jewel herself "seemed shaped in snow," and Marlow felt as "chilled" as if he had entered "the cold abode of despair" (p. 348).

20. Royal Roussel, in *The Metaphysics of Darkness: A Study in the Unity and Development of Conrad's Fiction* (Baltimore: The Johns Hopkins University Press, 1971), p. 93, suggests that Jewel might be Stein's daughter. More recently Elizabeth Brody Tenenbaum, in " 'And

the Woman is Dead Now': A Reconsideration of Conrad's Stein," *Studies in the Novel* 10 (1978), 335-45, fully argues the same hypothesis and points out how this hypothesis, if valid, gives "tremendous force" (p. 344) to the novel's conclusion.

21. The quotation is from Albert J. Guerard, *Conrad the Novelist* (1958; rpt. New York: Atheneum, 1967), p. 145, but the idea was first argued by Gustav Morf in *The Polish Heritage of Joseph Conrad* (London: Sampson, Low, and Marston, 1930), pp. 157-58. Daleski (p. 101), however, points out that "Brown's insinuation of their 'common guilt' . . . forces Jim not so much to an identification as to a recognition that the disreputable outlaw is in fact a better man . . . for he roundly asserts he would not do what Jim has done."

22. Raval, p. 403.

23. Guerard, p. 150.

24. Walter F. Wright, *Romance and Tragedy in Joseph Conrad* (Lincoln: University of Nebraska Press, 1949), p. 113.

25. Baines, p. 290.

26. Harry S. Epstein, "*Lord Jim* as a Tragic Action," *Studies in the Novel* 5 (1973), 242.

27. Epstein, p. 242.

28. Marlow, it might be noted, tries to argue that Jim's trust was appropriate because the "truth" of Brown's "story . . . seemed warranted by the rough frankness, by a sort of virile sincerity in accepting the morality and the consequences of his acts" (p. 394). It would seem that the story of Brown's most recent exploits — how he, thwarting an attempt to have him imprisoned, came, in a recently stolen Spanish schooner, to Patusan to steal supplies and anything else of value — should provide excellent reason for mistrusting him. So either Jim's trust rests on a lie or (and this is curious logic) a man honest about his dishonestry becomes honest in other respects too.

29. Paul Kirschner, *Conrad: The Psychologist as Artist* (Edinburgh: Oliver and Boyd, 1965), p. 58.

30. Watt, p. 6.

31. Zdzislaw Najder, "*Lord Jim:* A Romantic Tragedy of Honor," *Conradiana* 1, No. 1 (1968), 3.

32. Berthoud, p. 91.

33. Jackson W. Heimer, "Betrayal, Guilt, and Attempted Redemption in *Lord Jim,*" *Ball State University Forum* 9 (1968), 41.

34. Heimer, p. 42.

35. William J. Cook, Jr., "*Lord Jim* as Metaphor," *Conradiana* 1, No. 2 (1968-69), 47.

36. Alvin Greenberg, "Lord Jim and the Rock of Sisyphus," *Forum* 6, No. 3 (1968), 15.

37. Ira Sadoff, "Sartre and Conrad: Lord Jim as Existential Hero," *Dalhousie Review* 49 (1969), 525.

38. Bruce Johnson, *Conrad's Models of Mind* (Minneapolis: University of Minnesota Press, 1971), p. 60, emphasis in the original.

39. Said, p. 103.

40. As Raval observes, "Jim cannot see that martyrdom and courage have little significance since they are no longer distinguishable from suicide" (p. 404), and, more to the point, neither can Marlow.

41. Cheris Kramer, "Parallel Motives in *Lord Jim,*" *Conradiana* 2, No. 1 (1969), 58.

42. Johnson, p. 59.

43. Berthoud, p. 75.

44. David Daiches, *The Novel and the Modern World,* rev. ed. (Chicago: University of Chicago Press, 1960), p. 35.

45. Guerard, p. 134.

46. Theo Steinmann, in "Lord Jim's Progression Through Homology," *ARIEL: A Review of International English Literature* 5 (1974), 81-93, notes numerous ways in which Jim is unfavorably contrasted to Stein as well as to other characters in *Lord Jim.*

47. Watt, p. 11.

48. Robert R. Hodges, "The Four Fathers of Lord Jim," *University Review* 31 (1964), 105.

49. Tanner, p. 379.

50. My point here was convincing argued over twenty years ago by Guerard who observed that "the casual reader [and for Guerard "many professional critics are casual readers"] usually ignores or minimizes the important evidence *against* Lord Jim, . . . assumes that Conrad wholly approved of his hero, and is quite certain that Jim 'redeemed himself' in Patusan" (p. 131, italics in the original). But Guerard did not do what much subsequent apologist criticism suggests he might advantageously have done and fully examine the "evidence *against*" Jim that is dramatized in the novel. I would also here suggest that recent attempts to cast Marlow as the redeeming hero of the novel also do so in the face of considerable contrary evidence. Paul Bruss, for example, in "*Lord Jim:* The Maturing of Marlow," *Conradiana* 7 (1976), argues that the "stunning achievement" of "Marlow's maturation" comes as he tells his first story of Jim (p. 25). Consequently, that tale is not " 'incomplete' as the unidentified listener suggests," for it is Marlow's "fully detailed" account of his own "spectacular maturation" (p. 26). But the omniscient narrator in the novel also attests to the "incompleteness" of "that incomplete story" that Bruss would make whole. The final section of the novel cannot be, then, as Bruss suggests, a kind of addendum that "merely disclose[s] Jim's fate, his failure to mature," and thereby "sharply contrasts" Marlow's story with Jim's (p. 26). As I have shown, these two tales are far too interconnected to be thus divided and set one against the other. Moreover, as Said rightly insists, "Marlow's generosity toward Jim is rooted in precisely that same tendency to romantic projection because of which Jim so embarrassingly prefers courageous voyages in projective inspiration to voyages in actuality" (pp. 102-3).

51. Raval, p. 389.

52. Daniel R. Schwarz, "The Journey to Patusan: The Education of Jim and Marlow in Conrad's *Lord Jim,*" *Studies in the Novel* 4 (1972), 442-43.

53. Raval, p. 391.

54. Raval, pp. 389 and 391.

55. Numerous critics have observed that Jim is, in this broadest sense, "one of us." An early example is Wallace Stegner who, in "Variations on a Theme by Conrad," *Yale Review* 39

(1950), 514, observes that Conrad's protagonist becomes "man upon the earth." Carrying that idea one step further, Dorothy Van Ghent, in *The English Novel* (1953; rpt. New York: Harper and Row, 1967), p. 277, maintains that "the enigma" in *Lord Jim* "is not what Jim is but what we are."

56. Miller, p. 40.

Chapter 2

1. *Nostromo,* Canterbury Edition, Vol. 9 (New York: Doubleday and Page, 1924), p. 511. Subsequent references to this edition will be made parenthetically in the text.

2. H.M. Daleski, *Joseph Conrad: The Way of Dispossession* (New York: Holmes and Meier, 1976), p. 121.

3. Captain Mitchell correctly notes the ingratitude of the rich and comments on the incongruity of a man whose fortune was saved because of Nostromo later complaining about Nostromo cadging cigars, but Nostromo's prerevolutionary employer does not know that his Capataz has secretly rewarded himself by deciding to confiscate the silver.

4. William W. Bonney, "Joseph Conrad and the Discontinuous Point of View," *The Journal of Narrative Technique* 2 (1972), 110.

5. As Edward W. Said, in *Beginnings: Intention and Method* (Baltimore: The Johns Hopkins University Press, 1975), p. 101, dryly observes, "Mitchell has little sense of the complexity with which his artless narrative has been coping," and thus this character particularly serves to point the reader to a deeper understanding than his own.

6. Gareth Jenkins, "Conrad's *Nostromo* and History," *Literature and History* No. 5 (1977), p. 174.

7. Robert F. Haugh, *Joseph Conrad: Discovery in Design* (Norman: University of Oklahoma Press, 1957), pp. 154-55.

8. Rosemary Freeman, "Conrad's *Nostromo:* A Source and Its Use," *Modern Fiction Studies* 7 (1961-62), 325.

9. Norman Sherry, *Conrad's Western World* (Cambridge, Eng.: Cambridge University Press, 1971), p. 169.

10. Irving Howe, *Politics and the Novel* (New York: Meridian, 1957), p. 112.

11. Albert J. Guerard, *Conrad the Novelist* (1958; rpt. New York: Atheneum, 1967), p. 200. Jackson W. Heimer, in his "Betrayal, Confession, Attempted Redemption, and Punishment in *Nostromo,*" *Texas Studies in Literature and Language* 8 (1966-67), 569, also observes that "the omniscient narrator, so often harsh and sardonic with this boulevardier, drops many skeptical comments himself"; and still more recently Jeffrey Berman, in *Joseph Conrad: Writing as Rescue* (New York: Astra Books, 1977), p. 93, notes "the authorial authenticity of Decoud's voice."

12. Joyce Carol Oates, "The Tragedy of *Nostromo,*" *Novel* 9 (1975), 11.

13. Oates, p. 13. Guerard earlier made the same suggestion that "Conrad may be condeming Decoud for a withdrawal and skepticism more radical than Decoud ever shows; which are, in fact, Conrad's own" (p. 199).

14. C.B. Cox, *Joseph Conrad: The Modern Imagination* (London: Dent, 1974), p. 81.

15. Alan Friedman, *The Turn of the Novel: The Transition to Modern Fiction* (New York: Oxford University Press, 1966), p. 91.
16. Guerard, p. 202.
17. Berman, p. 98.
18. Harry Marten, "Conrad's Skeptic Reconsidered: A Study of Martin Decoud," *Nineteenth-Century Fiction* 27 (1972), 86.
19. William W. Bonney, *Thorns and Arabesques: Contexts for Conrad's Fiction* (Baltimore: The Johns Hopkins University Press, 1980), p. 114.
20. Friedman, p. 91.
21. Friedman, p. 93.
22. Juliet McLaughlan, *Conrad:* Nostromo, Studies in English Literature, No. 40 (London: Edward Arnold, 1969), p. 38.
23. Daniel R. Schwarz, "Conrad's Quarrel with Politics: The Disrupted Family in *Nostromo,*" *University of Toronto Quarterly* 47 (1977), 40.
24. Said, p. 107.
25. Eloise Knapp Hay, *The Political Novels of Joseph Conrad* (Chicago: University of Chicago Press, 1963), p. 203.
26. Peter Christmas, "Conrad's *Nostromo:* A Tale of Europe," *Literature and History* 6 (1980), 69.
27. Friedman, p. 94.
28. Guerard, p. 203; and G.W. Spence, "The Form of Part III of *Nostromo,*" *Conradiana* 3, No. 1 (1970-71), 81.
29. Leo Gurko, *Joseph Conrad: Giant in Exile* (New York: Macmillan, 1962), p. 133.
30. Dr. Monygham, "living on the inexhaustible treasure of his devotion drawn upon in the secret of his heart like a store of unlawful wealth" (p. 504), is, perhaps, the exception who proves the rule. But even in his case love remains problematic. It is first, as he admits, unlawful and, also, it does not fully redeem him. Even though the figure of Father Beron no longer haunts his dreams, Dr. Monygham is too intent on knowing of Nostromo's possible failure for the reader to believe that he has completely come to terms with his own.
31. Jacques Berthoud, *Joseph Conrad: The Major Phase* (Cambridge, Eng.: Cambridge University Press, 1978), p. 126.
32. Lee M. Whitehead, in "*Nostromo:* The Tragic 'Idea,' " *Nineteenth-Century Fiction* 23 (1968-69), 469, argues that one of Nostromo's "motives for the ride to Cayta" is to "carry out [Teresa's] last injuction: 'save the children,' " but action in *Nostromo*, he points out, regularly "leads to its own negation." In keeping with this principle, "Nostromo is to betray those children he saved, Linda to Giselle, and Giselle to the treasure." Betraying the children, he also betrays the mother.
33. Edward W. Said, "Conrad/*Nostromo:* Record and Reality," in John Unterecker, ed., *Approaches to the Twentieth-Century Novel* (New York: Crowell, 1965), p. 124.
34. This topic is discussed in detail by Schwarz (pp. 37-55).

35. Said, "Conrad/*Nostromo,*" p. 150.

36. The dream of treasure is probably the more tragic dream. As Bruce Johnson, in *Conrad's Models of Mind* (Minneapolis: University of Minnesota Press, 1971), p. 117, observes "faith in another fallible human" may not be any "more secure" than other faiths, "but at least such intimate dependence defines one's humanity as Gould's and Nostromo's never can be."

37. Cox, p. 70.

38. Howe, p. 106, emphasis in the original.

39. Royal Roussel, *The Metaphysics of Darkness: A Study in the Unity and Development of Conrad's Fiction* (Baltimore: The Johns Hopkins University Press, 1971), p. 130.

40. Conrad, in this respect, is true to his sources. Sherry (p. 351) observes: "What does strike one in reading about South American affairs of the period is the repetitive nature of the experience one is discovering."

41. Winifred Lynskey, "The Role of the Silver in *Nostromo,*" *Modern Fiction Studies* 1 (1955), 21.

42. More, however, is involved than a perpetual repetition of the past. As Avrom Fleishman, in *The English Historical Novel: Walter Scott to Virginia Woolf* (Baltimore: The Johns Hopkins University Press, 1971), p. 232, argues: "*Nostromo* does not predict the form of the future, yet it is perhaps the only novel of history to project an anticipation of the future as successfully as it does a sense of the past."

43. Christmas, p. 79.

Chapter 3

1. Jackson W. Heimer, "Betrayal in *The Secret Agent,*" *Conradiana* 7 (1976), 245.

2. Heimer, pp. 245 and 247.

3. The brief quotations are, in order, from Jack Shadoian, "Irony Triumphant: Verloc's Death," *Conradiana* 3, No. 2 (1971), 86; C.B. Cox, *Joseph Conrad: The Modern Imagination* (London: Dent, 1974), p. 85; and Peter Stine, "Conrad's Secrets in *The Secret Agent,*" *Conradiana* 13 (1981), p. 125.

4. F.R. Leavis, *The Great Tradition: George Eliot, Henry James, and Joseph Conrad* (London: Chatto and Windus, 1948), p. 209.

5. J. Hillis Miller, *Poets of Reality: Six Twentieth-Century Writers* (1965, rpt. New York: Atheneum, 1969), p. 43.

6. H.M. Daleski, *Joseph Conrad: The Way of Dispossession* (New York: Holmes and Meier, 1976), p. 151.

7. J.H. Retinger, *Conrad and His Contemporaries* (London: Minerva, 1941), p. 91.

8. *The Secret Agent,* Canterbury Edition, Vol. 13 (New York: Doubleday and Page, 1924), p. 93. Subsequent references to this edition will be made parenthetically in the text.

9. Joseph Wiesenfarth, "Stevie and the Structure of *The Secret Agent,*" *Modern Fiction Studies* 13 (1967), 514.

10. Leo Gurko, *Joseph Conrad: Giant in Exile* (New York: Macmillan, 1962), p. 171. Jonathan Arac, in "Romanticism, the Self, and the City: *The Secret Agent* in Literary History," *Boundary* 29, No. 1 (1980), 75-90, discusses in much more detail and different terminology the novel as a romantic portrait of man in the modern city.

11. Jacques Berthoud, *Joseph Conrad: The Major Phase* (Cambridge, Eng.: Cambridge University Press, 1978), p. 150.

12. Mark Conray, in "The Panoptical City: The Structure of Suspicion in *The Secret Agent,*" *Conradiana* 15 (1983), 203-17, stresses, in somewhat different terms, the role of "misinformation" in the novel.

13. Miller, pp. 40-41.

14. Daleski, p. 157. In contrast to Daleski, however, a number of commentators uncritically approve of Winnie. For example, Eloise Knapp Hay, in *The Political Novels of Joseph Conrad* (Chicago: University of Chicago Press, 1963), p. 256, refers to Winnie as a "thoroughbred in fortitude, reticence, and self-denial"; while Norman N. Holland, in "Style as Character: *The Secret Agent,*" *Modern Fiction Studies* 12 (1966), 225, sees her as a "paragon of self-sacrifice." A close examination of Winnie's acts and motives does not sustain such judgments. Her marriage represents, as James Walton points out in "Conrad and Naturalism: *The Secret Agent,*" *Texas Studies in Literature and Language* 9 (1967), 298, "not self-sacrifice," but "clearly ... a 'respectable' ... form of prostitution."

15. As Stine observes of Stevie's drawing of "innumerable circles": "These 'whirling circles' have many valences" (p. 135).

16. Verloc's comment, of course, looks both backward to his brother-in-law's death and, with obvious irony, forward to his own.

17. John Hagan, "The Design of Conrad's *The Secret Agent,*" *ELH* 22 (1955), 155.

18. Paul Kirschner, *Conrad: The Psychologist as Artist* (Edinburgh: Oliver and Boyd, 1968), p. 79.

19. David Daiches, *The Novel and the Modern World,* rev. ed. (Chicago: University of Chicago Press, 1960), p. 56.

20. Daiches, p. 57.

21. Claire Rosenfield, *Paradise of Snakes: An Archetypal Analysis of Conrad's Political Novels* (Chicago: University of Chicago Press, 1967), p. 109.

22. Daiches, p. 57.

23. David L. Kubal, "*The Secret Agent* and the Mechanical Chaos," *Bucknell Review* 15, No. 3 (1967), 75, provides one example. He maintains that Verloc's false trust in domesticity and in Winnie's love rendered him "unable to fend off her feeble approach with the knife." (But nothing in the novel suggests her approach was feeble.) Albert J. Guerard, in *Conrad the Novelist* (1958, rpt. New York: Atheneum, 1967), p. 230, is even more severe. "The misunderstanding is caused not by misinformation but by vanity, and Verloc rather than his wife takes the initiative in each important step towards his murder." (The text does not fully support this interpretation either.)

24. R.W. Stallman, in "Time and *The Secret Agent,*" in R.W. Stallman, ed., *The Art of Joseph Conrad: A Critical Symposium* (East Lansing: Michigan State University Press, 1960), p. 243, notes the irony of Winnie's rejecting a butcher for a husband and later butchering her husband.

25. For a fuller discussion of illusion and duplicity in the family relationship of the Verlocs see Arnold E. Davidson, "The Sign of Conrad's Secret Agent," *College Literature* 8 (1981), 33-41.

26. As Berthoud notes, "Verloc cannot be held solely responsible for not knowing what his wife thinks and feels, for she is in her own way as impenetrable as he is" (p. 150).

27. The argument advanced here is carried considerably further by Jack I. Biles in "Winnie Verloc: Agent of Death," *Conradiana* 13 (1981), 101-8.

28. The brief quotations are, in order, from Christopher Cooper, *Conrad and the Human Dilemma* (London: Chatto and Windus, 1970), p. 52; and Stine, p. 129.

29. This point is argued more fully in Arnold E. Davidson, "The Open Ending of *The Secret Agent,*" *ARIEL: A Review of International English Literature* 7 (1976), 84-100; Daleski also observes that "it is madness, not a mystical or poetic justice, that accounts for [Winnie's] resemblance to Stevie as she moves [to kill] Verloc" (p. 148).

30. Leavis, p. 215.

31. Albert Cook, *The Meaning of Fiction* (Detroit: Wayne State University Press, 1960), p. 205, sees the novel as "a chain reaction of murders." Miller more accurately describes the plot as "a chain reaction, a sequence of disenchantments started by M. Vladimir" (p. 45).

32. E.M.W. Tillyard, "*The Secret Agent* Reconsidered." *Essays in Criticism* 11 (1961), 301.

33. Thomas B. Gilmore, Jr., "Retributive Irony in Conrad's *The Secret Agent,*" *Conradiana* 1, No. 3 (1969), 44.

34. For an excellent discussion of the deluding rationalizations with which the Inspector attempts to justify his intentions see D.R.C. Marsh, "Moral Judgments in *The Secret Agent,*" *English Studies in Africa,* (1960), 60-62.

35. Lynne Cheney, in "Joseph Conrad's *The Secret Agent* and Graham Greene's *It's A Battlefield:* A Study in Structural Meaning," *Modern Fiction Studies* 16 (1970), 117-31, observed that the rational orderliness of society is not too firmly upheld when it depends on men like Sir Ethelred or Inspector Heat.

36. Some critics exercise considerable ingenuity in attempting to read the novel affirmatively. Hay, for example (p. 255), maintains that solid British institutions forestall any possible triumph of anarchy. Even the almshouse to which Winnie's mother commits herself, "however depressing, is as trustworthy as the corner policeman." Since the almshouse is portrayed as a foretaste of the grave and a policeman as the equivalent of a thief, Hay's observations may be true but not in the sense intended. But perhaps the most extreme attempt to discover positive values in *The Secret Agent* is seen in Sister Jane Marie Luecke's "Conrad's Secret and Its Agent," *Modern Fiction Studies* 10 (1964), 47. Even the occasional shining of the sun proves, for this critic, that "disorder and darkness are consequent on man's shutting out the sun from his life" and thus refusing to see "the presence of what is permanently ordered and beautifully permanent."

37. Jeffrey Berman, *Joseph Conrad: Writing as Rescue* (New York: Astra Books, 1977), p. 125.

38. Joseph I. Fradin, "Anarchist, Detective, and Saint: The Possibilities of Action in *The Secret Agent,*" *PMLA* 83 (1968), 1415.

39. Jacques Darras, *Joseph Conrad and the West: Signs of Empire* (London: Macmillan, 1982), p. 106.

40. Stallman, pp. 234-54.

41. Kubal, pp. 65-77.

42. For an excellent discussion of the way in which Conrad handles time in this novel see Avrom Fleishman, *Conrad's Politics: Community and Anarchy in The Fiction of Joseph Conrad* (Baltimore: The Johns Hopkins University Press, 1967), pp. 203-12. As Fleishman points out, the anarchists seek to negate or abolish time. But even the most extreme anarchist, the Professor, "cannot transcend the limitations of human life which is lived in time" (p. 211).

43. Luecke, pp. 37-48.

44. Holland, p. 222.

45. Daleski, p. 159.

46. Joseph I. Fradin, "Conrad's Everyman: *The Secret Agent," Texas Studies in Literature and Language* 11 (1970), 1023.

Chapter 4

1. Albert J. Guerard, *Conrad the Novelist* (1958; rpt. New York: Atheneum, 1967), p. 232.

2. Frederick R. Karl, *A Reader's Guide to Joseph Conrad* (New York: Farrar, Straus and Giroux [Noonday], 1960), p. 222.

3. Karl, p. 224.

4. Karl, p. 223. John Hagan, in "Conrad's *Under Western Eyes:* The Question of Razumov's Guilt and Remorse," *Studies in the Novel* 1 (1969), 319, observes that Razumov finally discovers that he "can no longer endure the loneliness and self-hate of accepting trust on false premises, even if it is the trust of the revolutionists he despises" and that he has especially reached such a point after he has "confessed to Nathalie and . . . in effect made her his conscience."

5. Karl, p. 223.

6. Avrom Fleishman, *Conrad's Politics: Community and Anarchy in the Fiction of Joseph Conrad* (Baltimore: The Johns Hopkins University Press, 1967), p. 219.

7. Karl, p. 223.

8. Guerard, p. 245.

9. Penn R. Szittya, "Metafiction: The Double Narration in *Under Western Eyes," ELH* 48 (1981), 831.

10. Frank Kermode, "Secrets and Narrative Sequence," *Critical Inquiry* 7 (1980), 100.

11. Joseph Conrad, *Under Western Eyes,* Canterbury Edition, Vol. 22 (New York: Doubleday and Page, 1924), p. 382. Subsequent references to this edition will be made parenthetically in the text.

12. Jocelyn Baines, *Joseph Conrad: A Critical Biography* (London: Weidenfeld and Nicolson, 1960), p. 363.

13. Claire Rosenfield, *Paradise of Snakes: An Archetypal Analysis of Conrad's Political Novels* (Chicago: University of Chicago Press, 1967), p. 163.

14. George Goodin, "The Personal and the Political in *Under Western Eyes,*" *Nineteenth-Century Fiction* 25 (1970), 339.

15. Bruce Johnson, *Conrad's Models of Mind* (Minneapolis: University of Minnesota Press, 1971), p. 147.

16. Hagan documents the degree to which Razumov, for informing on Haldin, has been imperceptively condemned by numerous critics as an essentially selfish character who merits his subsequent fate. As Hagan points out, this reading "does violence to Conrad's considerable moral subtlety, reducing the novel perilously close to popular adventure and romance" (p. 311). Johnson has more recently noted that Razumov is not confronted by any simple moral choice, since "in aiding Haldin he would have betrayed himself fully as much as he has by reporting [Haldin] to the police" (p. 147).

17. Placing undue emphasis on the virtues of reason, Razumov goes on to suggest that the "thinking reed" should be considered superior to "the unthinking forces that are about to crush him out of existence." The consciousness of an asserted superiority must be, in such circumstances, singularly unsatisfying.

18. Christopher Cooper, *Conrad and the Human Dilemma* (London: Chatto and Windus, 1970), p. 69.

19. Hagan, p. 317.

20. Tony Tanner, "Nightmare and Complacency: Razumov and the Western Eye," *The Critical Quarterly* 4 (1962), 205.

21. Tanner, p. 207.

22. Guerard, p. 240.

23. J.I.M. Stewart, *Joseph Conrad* (New York: Dodd Mead, 1968), p. 207.

24. John E. Saveson, "The Moral Discovery of *Under Western Eyes,*" *Criticism* 14 (1972), 35.

25. Ted E. Boyle, in *Symbol and Meaning in the Fiction of Joseph Conrad* (The Hague: Mouton, 1965), p. 208, observes that "Mikulin is obviously an older Razumov."

26. Robert Secor, "The Function of the Narrator in *Under Western Eyes,*" *Conradiana* 3, No. 1 (1971), 30.

27. Hagan, p. 313.

28. Jeffrey Berman, *Joseph Conrad: Writing as Rescue* (New York: Astra Books, 1977), p. 144.

29. And certainly the reader need not accept Maureen Frie's suggestion, in "Feminism — Antifeminism in *Under Western Eyes,*" *Conradiana* 5, No. 2 (1973), 62, that "Conrad stresses again and again Nathalie's androgynous nature, which combines the best qualities of both sexes." It is not Conrad but his narrator who insists, rather dubiously, on androgynous formulations. Conrad clearly shows that Nathalie hardly merits the praise lavished upon her and does not at all embody some androgynous ideal.

30. Harriet Gilliam, in "The Daemonic in Conrad's *Under Western Eyes,*" *Conradiana* 9 (1977), 230, makes much this same point when she observes that "ultimately it is [the narrator's] very defenses that entrap him." For further analysis of the limitations of both the narrator and his western perspective, see also Gilliam's "Vision in Conrad's *Under Western Eyes,*" *Texas Studies in Language and Literature* 19 (1977), 24-41, and "Russia and the West in Conrad's *Under Western Eyes,*" *Studies in the Novel* 10 (1978), 218-33.

31. Secor, p. 36.

32. C.B. Cox, *Joseph Conrad: The Modern Imagination* (London: Dent, 1974), p. 107.

33. Rosenfield, p. 159.

34. Jackson W. Heimer, "The Betrayer as Intellectual: Conrad's *Under Western Eyes," Polish Review* 12, No. 4 (1967), p. 68.

35. Yet Fleishman, in *Conrad's Politics,* can still assert that "Razumov is found at the close of the novel in the role of a patron saint of the revolutionists" (p. 237). Neither the novel nor Fleishman provides any substantial basis for this assertion. More recently, however, Fleishman has modified this positive view of Razumov's final condition. In *Fiction and the Ways of Knowing: Essays on British Novels* (Austin: University of Texas Press, 1978), p. 135, he observes that Razumov "is still very much alone" at the novel's end, and even if he has become "a communal oracle, . . . this may be only a new form of alienation."

36. For discerning discussions of the similarities and differences between the two novels, see Baines, pp. 369-70; and Andrzej Busza, "Rhetoric and Ideology in Conrad's *Under Western Eyes,"* in *Joseph Conrad: A Commemoration,* ed. Norman Sherry (London: Macmillan, 1976), pp. 105-18.

37. Baines, p. 369.

38. Conrad himself, in a letter to Edward Garnett reprinted in Edward Garnett, ed., *Letters from Joseph Conrad, 1895-1924* (Indianapolis: Bobbs-Merrill, 1928), pp. 232-33, asked: "Is it possible that you haven't seen that in this book I am concerned with nothing but ideas, to the exclusion of everything else?"

39. Fleishman, *Conrad's Politics,* pp. 222-23.

40. Tanner, p. 213.

41. Edward Wasiolek, *Dostoevsky: The Major Fiction* (Cambridge, Mass.: Massachusetts Institute of Technology Press, 1964), p. 67.

42. Wasiolek, p. 84.

43. Tanner, p. 214.

Chapter 5

1. *Victory,* Canterbury Edition, Vol. 15 (New York: Doubleday and Page, 1924), p. 90. Subsequent references to this edition will be made parenthetically in the text.

2. Gary Geddes, *Conrad's Later Novels* (Montreal: McGill-Queens University Press, 1980), p. 42.

3. J.I.M. Stewart, *Joseph Conrad* (New York: Dodd Mead, 1968), pp. 220-21.

4. As Donald A. Dike observes, in "The Tempest of Axel Heyst," *Nineteenth-Century Fiction* 17 (1962), 100, "The method of [*Victory*] makes a point of general doubt and uncertainty, darkened understanding and glib misunderstanding."

5. However, as Bruce Johnson, in *Conrad's Models of Mind* (Minneapolis: University of Minnesota Press, 1971), p. 161, points out, although "Heyst claims that his reasons for abandoning what we ordinarily think of as life are purely rational," Conrad suggests that Heyst "does not reach the decision to drift, to disengage from life, solely as an intellectual matter."

6. F.R. Leavis, *The Great Tradition: George Eliot, Henry James, and Joseph Conrad* (London: Chatto and Windus, 1948), p. 66.

7. The brief quotation is from Geddes, p. 44.

8. Johnson, p. 163.

9. Jeffrey Berman, *Joseph Conrad: Writing as Rescue* (New York: Astra Books, 1972), p. 172.

10. Robert F. Haugh, *Joseph Conrad: Discovery in Design* (Norman: University of Oklahoma Press, 1957), p. 112.

11. Norman Page, "Dickensian Elements in *Victory,*" *Conradiana* 5, No. 1 (1973), 40.

12. Leo Gurko, *Joseph Conrad: Giant in Exile* (New York: Macmillan, 1962), p. 217.

13. George F. Reinecke, in "Conrad's *Victory:* Psychomachy, Christian Symbols, and Theme," in Rima D. Reck, ed., *Explorations of Literature,* Louisiana State University Studies, Humanity Services, No. 18 (Baton Rouge: Louisiana State University Press, 1966), pp. 70-80, notes several parallels between Mr. Jones and Heyst's father, the most obvious being the fact that they both characteristically wear blue robes.

14. Jeffrey Meyers, *Homosexuality and Literature 1890-1930* (London: University of London Athlone Press, 1977), p. 88. Meyers fully examines the evidence of Heyst's confused sexual orientation but also points out that "the sexual relationships of all the characters remain ambiguous" (p. 77). More recently, however, Suresh Raval, in "Conrad's *Victory:* Skepticism and Experience," *Nineteenth-Century Fiction* 34 (1980), 418, has argued that "Heyst's primary bond with Jones" is "his skepticism," which, in each man, takes the form of a "contempt for life" and for women.

15. John A. Palmer, *Joseph Conrad's Fiction: A Study in Literary Growth* (Ithaca: Cornell University Press, 1968), p. 178.

16. Adam Gillon, in "Joseph Conrad and Shakespeare, Part Four: A Reading of *Victory,*" *Conradiana* 7 (1976), observes that "Conrad's use of Shakespearean archetypes . . . reaches a culminating point in *Victory.*" He goes on to elucidate numerous parallels but overlooks one that seems particularly pertinent. Heyst, like Hamlet, must oppose a diabolic father figure but to dispose of the parodic father is perhaps to become like him.

17. Gurko, p. 220.

18. Frederick R. Karl, *A Reader's Guide to Joseph Conrad* (New York: Farrar, Straus and Giroux [Noonday], 1960), p. 256.

19. Geddes, pp. 49-50.

20. Bernard C. Meyer, *Joseph Conrad: A Psychoanalytical Biography* (Princeton: Princeton University Press, 1967), p. 297.

21. Wilfred S. Dowden, *Joseph Conrad: The Imagined Style* (Nashville: Vanderbilt University Press, 1970), notes how, with *Victory*, Conrad parodies numerous Biblical passages "in his development of an ironic theme, a *reductio ad absurdum* of Christianity" (p. 157).

22. Thomas Moser, *Joseph Conrad: Achievement and Decline* (Cambridge, Mass.: Harvard University Press, 1957), p. 117, early noted that "we are surely justified in seeing the knife as a phallic symbol."

23. Murray Kreiger, *The Tragic Vision* (Chicago: University of Chicago Press, 1960), p. 191.

24. Sharon Kaehele and Howard German, "Conrad's *Victory:* a Reassessment." *Modern Fiction Studies* 10 (1964), 55-72.

25. The brief quotation is from Stanton de Voren Hoffman, *Comedy and Form in the Fiction of Joseph Conrad* (The Hague: Mouton, 1969), pp. 130-31, who thus describes the assortment of weapons that Jones keeps close at hand. As this critic notes, there is an element of comical exaggeration in villains so completely armed, yet the guns remain problematically present.

26. Seymour L. Gross, "The Devil in Samburan: Jones and Ricardo in *Victory*," *Nineteenth-Century Fiction* 16 (1961), 84.

27. Kingsley Widmer, "Conrad's Pyrrhic Victory," *Twentieth-Century Literature* 5 (1959), 129.

28. As Raval observes: "There is no doubt that Heyst's final words encapsulate the general movement of the story, that they express Heyst's wish that he had 'learned' love and trust earlier in life. Yet, if placed in the total context of the novel, Heyst's words reveal a despair and bitterness that are powerful psychological adjuncts of his deep-seated skepticism" (p. 416). Denied "an illusory certainty stemming from the naiveté of youth and inexperience," Raval further argues (p. 416), Heyst almost necessarily commits suicide.

29. William W. Bonney, *Thorns and Arabesques: Contexts for Conrad's Fiction* (Baltimore: The Johns Hopkins University Press, 1980), p. 187.

30. Ian Watt, *Conrad in the Nineteenth Century* (Berkeley and Los Angeles: University of California Press, 1981), p. 175. See also Cedric Watts, *A Preface to Conrad* (London: Longman, 1982), pp. 116-17.

Bibliography

Adams, Robert M. *Strains of Discord: Studies in Literary Openness.* Ithaca: Cornell University Press, 1958.

Allen, Jerry. *The Sea Years of Joseph Conrad.* New York: Doubleday, 1965.

———. *The Thunder and the Sunshine: A Biography of Joseph Conrad.* New York: Putnam's, 1958.

Andreas, Osborne. *Joseph Conrad: A Study in Non-Conformity.* New York: Philosophical Library, 1959.

Aubrey, Georges Jean. *Joseph Conrad: Life and Letters,* 2 vols. New York: Doubleday, 1927.

———. *The Sea Dreamer: A Definitive Biography of Joseph Conrad.* Translated by Helen Sebba. New York: Doubleday, 1957.

Baines, Jocelyn. *Joseph Conrad: A Critical Biography.* London: Weidenfeld and Nicolson, 1960.

Berman, Jeffrey. *Joseph Conrad: Writing as Rescue.* New York: Astra Books, 1977.

Berthoud, Jacques. *Joseph Conrad: The Major Phase.* Cambridge, Eng.: Cambridge University Press, 1978.

Bonney, William W. *Thorns and Arabesques: Contexts for Conrad's Fiction.* Baltimore: The Johns Hopkins University Press, 1980.

Booth, Wayne C. *The Rhetoric of Fiction.* Chicago: University of Chicago Press, 1961.

Boyle Ted E. *Symbol and Meaning in the Fiction of Joseph Conrad.* The Hague: Mouton, 1965.

Bradbrook, M.C. *Joseph Conrad: Poland's English Genius.* Cambridge, Eng.: Cambridge University Press, 1942.

Brown, E.K. *Rhythm in the Novel.* Toronto: University of Toronto Press, 1950.

Bruss, Paul. *Conrad's Early Sea Fiction: The Novelist as Navigator.* Lewisburg: Bucknell University Press, 1979.

Cook, Albert. *The Meaning of Fiction.* Detroit: Wayne State University Press, 1960.

Cooper, Christopher. *Conrad and the Human Dilemma.* London: Chatto and Windus, 1970.

Cox, C.B. *Joseph Conrad: The Modern Imagination.* London: Dent, 1974.

Crankshaw, Edward. *Joseph Conrad: Some Aspects of the Art of the Novel.* London: John Lane, 1936.

Curle, Richard. *Joseph Conrad and his Characters.* London: Heinemann, 1957.

Daiches, David. *The Novel and the Modern World.* Chicago: University of Chicago Press, 1939.

Daleski, H.M. *Joseph Conrad: The Way of Dispossession.* New York: Holmes and Meier, 1976.

Darras, Jacques. *Joseph Conrad and the West: Signs of Empire.* London: Macmillan, 1982.

Dowden, Wilfred S. *Joseph Conrad: The Imagined Style.* Nashville: Vanderbilt University Press, 1970.

Fleishman, Avrom. *Conrad's Politics: Community and Anarchy in the Fiction of Joseph Conrad.* Baltimore: The Johns Hopkins University Press, 1967.

———. *The English Historical Novel: Walter Scott to Virginia Woolf.* Baltimore: The Johns Hopkins University Press, 1971.

———. *Fiction and the Ways of Knowing: Essays on British Novels*. Austin: University of Texas Press, 1978.
Follett, Wilson, *Joseph Conrad: A Short Study of His Intellectual and Emotional Attitude Toward His Work and of the Chief Characteristics of His Novels*. Garden City: Doubleday Page, 1915.
Ford, Ford Madox. *Joseph Conrad: A Personal Remembrance*. Boston: Little Brown, 1924.
Forster, E.M. *Aspects of the Novel*. New York: Harcourt, Brace, 1927.
Friedman, Alan. *The Turn of the Novel: The Transition to Modern Fiction*. New York: Oxford University Press, 1966.
Geddes, Gary. *Conrad's Later Novels*. Montreal: McGill-Queens University Press, 1980.
Gekoski, R.A. *Conrad: The Moral World of the Novelist*. London: Paul Elak, 1978.
Gillon, Adam. *Conrad and Shakespeare and Other Essays*. New York: Astra Books, 1976.
———. *The Eternal Solitary: A Study of Joseph Conrad*. New York: Bookman Associates, 1960.
Glassman, Peter J. *Language and Being: Joseph Conrad and the Literature of Personality*. New York: Columbia University Press, 1976.
Gordon, John D. *Joseph Conrad: The Making of a Novelist*. Cambridge, Mass.: Harvard University Press, 1940.
Grossvogel, David I. *Limits of the Novel: Evolution of a Form from Chaucer to Robbe-Grillet*. Ithaca: Cornell University Press, 1968.
Guerard, Albert J. *Conrad the Novelist*. Cambridge, Mass.: Harvard University Press, 1958.
Guetti, James. *The Limits of Metaphor: A Study of Melville, Conrad, and Faulkner*. Ithaca: Cornell University Press, 1967.
Gurko, Leo. *Joseph Conrad: Giant in Exile*. New York: Macmillan, 1962.
———. *The Two Lives of Joseph Conrad*. New York: Crowell, 1965.
Hardy, Barbara. *The Appropriate Form: An Essay on the Novel*. London: University of London Press, 1964.
Haugh, Robert F. *Joseph Conrad: Discovery in Design*. Norman: University of Oklahoma Press, 1957.
Hawthorn, Jeremy. *Joseph Conrad: Language and Fictional Self-Consciousness*. London: Edward Arnold, 1979.
Hay, Eloise Knapp. *The Political Novels of Joseph Conrad*. Chicago: University of Chicago Press, 1963.
Hewitt, Douglas. *Conrad: A Reassessment*. 2d. ed. Chester Springs, Pa.: Dufour Editions, 1969.
Hoffman, Stanton de Voren. *Comedy and Form in the Fiction of Joseph Conrad*. The Hague: Mouton, 1969.
Howe, Irving. *Politics and the Novel*. New York: Meridian, 1957.
James, Henry. *The Art of Fiction and Other Essays*. Edited by M. Roberts. New York: Oxford University Press, 1948.
Johnson, Bruce. *Conrad's Models of Mind*. Minneapolis: University of Minnesota Press, 1971.
Karl, Frederick R. *Joseph Conrad: The Three Lives, a Biography*. New York: Farrar, Straus, and Giroux, 1979.
———. *A Reader's Guide to Joseph Conrad*. New York: Farrar, Straus, and Giroux (Noonday), 1960.
Kermode, Frank. *The Sense of an Ending: Studies in the Theory of Fiction*. New York: Oxford University Press, 1967.
Kirschner, Paul. *Conrad: The Psychologist as Artist*. Edinburgh: Oliver and Boyd, 1965.
La Bossière, Camille. *Joseph Conrad and the Science of Unknowing*. Fredericton, N.B.: York Press, 1979.
Leavis, F.R. *The Great Tradition: George Eliot, Henry James, and Joseph Conrad*. London: Chatto and Windus, 1948.

Liddell, Robert. *A Treatise on the Novel.* London: Cape, 1947.

———. *Some Principles of Fiction.* Bloomington: Indiana University Press, 1954.

Lubbock, Percy. *The Craft of Fiction.* London: Cape, 1921.

McClure, John A. *Kipling and Conrad: The Colonial Fiction.* Cambridge, Mass.: Harvard University Press, 1981.

McLaughlin, Juliet. *Conrad:* Nostromo. Studied in English Literature, no. 40. London: Edward Arnold, 1969.

Megroz, R.L. *Joseph Conrad's Mind and Method: A Study of Personality in Art.* London: Faber, 1931.

Miller, J. Hillis. *Fiction and Repetition: Seven English Novels.* Cambridge, Mass.: Harvard University Press, 1982.

———. *The Forms of Victorian Fiction.* Notre Dame: University of Notre Dame Press, 1968.

———. *Poets of Reality: Six Twentieth-Century Writers.* Cambridge, Mass.: Harvard University Press, 1965.

Morf, Gustav. *The Polish Heritage of Joseph Conrad.* London: Sampson, Low, and Marston, 1930.

Moser, Thomas. *Joseph Conrad: Achievement and Decline.* Cambridge, Mass.: Harvard University Press, 1957.

Mudrick, Marvin, ed. *Conrad: A Collection of Critical Essays.* Englewood Cliffs, N.J.: Prentice-Hall, 1966.

Richter, David H. *Fable's End: Completeness and Closure in Rhetorical Fiction.* Chicago: The University of Chicago Press, 1974.

Rosenfield, Claire. *Paradise of Snakes: An Archetypal Analysis of Conrad's Political Novels.* Chicago: University of Chicago Press, 1967.

Roussel, Royal. *The Metaphysics of Darkness: A Study in the Unity and Development of Conrad's Fiction.* Baltimore: The Johns Hopkins University Press, 1971.

Said, Edward W. *Beginnings: Intention and Method.* Baltimore: The Johns Hopkins University Press, 1975.

———. *Joseph Conrad and the Fiction of Autobiography.* Cambridge, Mass.: Harvard University Press, 1966.

Saveson, John E. *Joseph Conrad: The Making of a Moralist.* Amsterdam: Rodopi NV, 1972.

Scholes, Robert. *Approaches to the Novel.* San Francisco: Chandler, 1961.

———. *Elements of Fiction.* New York: Oxford University Press, 1968.

——— and Robert Kellogg. *The Nature of Narrative.* New York: Oxford University Press, 1966.

Schwarz, Daniel R. *Conrad:* Almayer's Folly *to* Under Western Eyes. Ithaca: Cornell University Press, 1980.

———. *Conrad: The Later Fiction.* London: Macmillan, 1982.

Secor, Robert. *The Rhetoric of Shifting Perspectives: Conrad's* Victory. Pennsylvania State University Studies, no. 32. University Park: The Pennsylvania State University, 1971.

Seltzer, Leon F. *The Vision of Melville and Conrad: A Comparative Study.* Athens: Ohio University Press, 1970.

Sherry, Norman, ed. *Conrad: The Critical Heritage.* London: Routledge and Kegan Paul, 1973.

———. *Conrad's Eastern World.* Cambridge, Eng.: Cambridge University Press, 1966.

———. *Conrad's Western World.* Cambridge, Eng.: Cambridge University Press, 1971.

———, ed. *Joseph Conrad: A Commemoration.* London: Macmillan, 1976.

Smith, Barbara Herrnstein. *Poetic Closure: A Study of How Poems End.* Chicago: University of Chicago Press, 1968.

Spencer, Sharon. *Space, Time, and Structure in the Modern Novel.* New York: New York University Press, 1971.

Stallman, Robert W., ed. *The Art of Joseph Conrad: A Critical Symposium.* East Lansing: Michigan State University Press, 1960.

Stewart, J.I.M. *Joseph Conrad.* New York: Dodd Mead, 1968.

Tanner, Tony. Lord Jim. Studies in English Literature, no. 12. London: Edward Arnold, 1963.

Thorburn, David. *Conrad's Romanticism.* New Haven: Yale University Press, 1974.

Torgovnick, Marianna. *Closure in the Novel.* Princeton: Princeton University Press, 1981.

Visiak, E.H. *The Mirror of Conrad.* New York: Philosophical Library, 1956.

Warner, Oliver. *Joseph Conrad.* London: Longmans, 1951.

Watt, Ian. *Conrad in the Nineteenth Century.* Berkeley and Los Angeles: University of California Press, 1979.

———, ed. The Secret Agent: *A Selection of Critical Essays.* London: Macmillan, 1973.

Watts, Cedric. *A Preface to Conrad.* London: Longman, 1982.

Wiley, Paul L. *Connrad's Measure of Man.* Madison: University of Wisconsin Press, 1954.

Wright, Walter F., ed. *Joseph Conrad on Fiction.* Lincoln: University of Nebraska Press, 1964.

———. *Romance and Tragedy in Joseph Conrad.* Lincoln: University of Nebraska Press, 1949.

Yelton, Donald Charles. *Mimesis and Metaphor: An Inquiry Into the Genesis and Scope of Conrad's Symbolic Imagery.* The Hague: Mouton, 1967.

Zabel, Morton Dauwen. *Craft and Character in Modern Fiction: Texts, Method, and Vocation.* New York: Viking, 1957.

Index

Baines, Jocelyn: on *Lord Jim,* 7,15,17; on *Under Western Eyes,* 72,85
Berman, Jeffrey: on *Nostromo,* 108n.11; on *Victory,* 91
Berthoud, Jacques: on *Lord Jim,* 25; on *The Secret Agent,* 57,112n.26
Bonney, William: on *Nostromo,* 33,40; on *Victory,* 101
Boyle, Ted: on *Lord Jim,* 8; on *Under Western Eyes,* 114n.25
Brautigan, Richard: *A Confederate General from Big Sur,* 5
Bruss, Paul: on *Lord Jim,* 8, 107n.50

Chance: compared to *Victory,* 87,88
Christmas, Peter: on *Nostromo,* 47-48
conclusion. *See* endings
Cooper, Christopher: on *Under Western Eyes,* 77
Cox, C. B.: on *Nostromo,* 37

Daiches, David, 3; on *Lord Jim,* 25; on *The Secret Agent,* 58-59
Daleski, H. M.: on *Nostromo,* 31; on *The Secret Agent,* 55
Darras, Jacques: on *The Secret Agent,* 68
Dickens, Charles: *Great Expectations,* 5
Dostoevsky, Fyodor: *Crime and Punishment,* 85-86

endings: closed, 2-3, 103n.10; Conrad's solution to, 5; defined, 1; multiple, 5; open, 2-4, 103n.10, 104nn.19,20
Epstein, Harry: on *Lord Jim,* 15-16

Fleishman, Avrom: on *Nostromo,* 110n.42; on *The Secret Agent,* 113n.42; on *Under Western Eyes,* 72,85,115n.35
Forster, E. M., 4
Fowles, John: *The French Lieutenant's Woman,* 5
Fradin, Joseph I.: on *The Secret Agent,* 68,69
Friedman, Alan, 3,4,103n.10,104n.19; on *Nostromo,* 37,43,44,48

Geddes, Gary: on *Victory,* 87,97
German, Howard: on *Victory,* 99
Gilmore, Thomas: on *The Secret Agent,* 67
Goodin, George: on *Under Western Eyes,* 75
Gose, Elliott: on *Lord Jim,* 7-8
Greenberg, Alvin: on *Lord Jim,* 23
Gross, Seymour: on *Victory,* 100
Guerard, Albert: on *Lord Jim,* 15,26,107n.50; on *Nostromo,* 36,48,108n.13; on *The Secret Agent,* 111n.23; on *Under Western Eyes,* 71,72,78
Gurko, Leo: on *Nostromo,* 48; on *Victory,* 96

Hagan, John: on *The Secret Agent,* 58; on *Under Western Eyes,* 72,77,113n.4,114n.16
Haugh, Robert: on *Lord Jim,* 7; on *Nostromo,* 34-35; on *Victory,* 91
Hay, Eloise: on *Nostromo,* 47; on *The Secret Agent,* 111n.14,112n.36
Heart of Darkness, 101
Heimer, Jackson: on *Lord Jim,* 22,23, 108n.11; on *Under Western Eyes,* 84,85
Holland, Norman, N.: on *The Secret Agent,* 69,111n.14
Howe, Irving: on *Nostromo,* 36,52
James, Henry: on endings, 4
Johnson, Bruce: on *Lord Jim,* 23; on *Nostromo,* 110n.36; on *Under Western Eyes,* 75,114n.16; on *Victory,* 88,115n.5
Johnson, Samuel: *Rasselas,* 4
Joyce, James: *Finnegans Wake,* 4

Kaehele, Sharon: on *Victory,* 99
Karl, Frederick: on *Under Western Eyes,* 71, 72; on *Victory,* 97
Kermode, Frank, 4; on *Under Western Eyes,* 72

Kirschner, Paul: on *Lord Jim,* 19; on *The Secret Agent,* 58
Kramer, Cheris: on *Lord Jim,* 24
Kreiger, Murray: on *Victory,* 99
Kubal, David: on *The Secret Agent,* 68, 111n.23

Leavis, F. R.: on *The Secret Agent,* 55,64; on *Victory,* 88
Lord Jim, 7-30,71; compared with *Nostromo,* 31; critics' interpretations of, 7-10,15-17, 19,20,22-26,28-30,103n.10,104nn.1,3, 105n.20,106n.21,107nn.40,50,55, 108nn.11,55; heroism in, 7-9
Lynskey, Winifred: on *Nostromo,* 53

McLaughlan, Juliet: on *Nostromo,* 47
Marten, Harry: on *Nostromo,* 40
Melville, Herman: *The Confidence Man,* 4
Meyers, Jeffrey: on *Victory,* 94, 116n.14
Miller, J. Hillis, 1,2; on *Lord Jim,* 30, 104nn.1,3; on *The Secret Agent,* 55,57,112n.31

Najder, Zdzislaw: on *Lord Jim,* 20
Nostromo, 31-53; compared with *Lord Jim,* 31; compared with *The Secret Agent,* 55,56; critics' interpretations of, 31,33-37, 40,43,44,47-48,51,52,108nn.11,13,109n.32, 110nn.36,42; "material interests" in, 31-32

Oates, Joyce Carol: on *Nostromo,* 36-37

Palmer, John: on *Victory,* 94

Raval, Suresh: on *Lord Jim,* 7,29,107n.40; on *Victory,* 116n.14, 117n.28
Richter, David H., 3-4
Rosenfield, Claire: on *The Secret Agent,* 59; on *Under Western Eyes,* 73

Sadoff, Ira: on *Lord Jim,* 23
Said, Edward: on *Lord Jim,* 9,23,107n.50; on *Nostromo,* 47,51,52,108n.5
Secor, Robert: on *Under Western Eyes,* 79-80
Secret Agent, The, betrayal in, 55-56; compared with *Nostromo,* 55,56; Conrad's opinion of, 55; critics' interpretations of, 53,55-59,64,67-69,111nn.10,12,14,23,24, 112nn.26,31,35,36,113n.42
Spence, G. W.: on *Nostromo,* 48
Stallman, R. W.: on *The Secret Agent,* 68,111n.24
Sterne, Laurence, 4
Stewart, J.I.M.: on *Under Western Eyes,* 78; on *Victory,* 87
Szittya, Penn: on *Under Western Eyes,* 72

Tanner, J. E.: on *Lord Jim,* 10,28; on *Under Western Eyes,* 86; on *Victory,* 87
Thompson, Commodore Sir Ivan: on *Lord Jim,* 8
Tillyard, E.M.W.: on *The Secret Agent,* 67
Torgovnick, Marianna: 1,2,103n.10

Under Western Eyes: compared to Conrad's other works, 71; compared to *Victory,* 87-89; critics' interpretations of, 71-73,75,77-80,84-86,113n.4,114nn.16,25, 29,30,115n.35; illusion in, 74-75

Victory: compared with *Chance,* 87-88; compared with *Under Western Eyes,* 87-89; critics' interpretations of, 87,88,91,94,96, 97,99-101,115nn.4,5,116nn.13,14,16,21,22, 117nn.25,28; plot summarized, 87-89

Watt, Ian: on *Lord Jim,* 8,19; on *Victory,* 101
Widmer, Kingsley: on *Victory,* 100
Wiesenfarth, Joseph: on *The Secret Agent,* 56
Wright, Walter: on *Lord Jim,* 15